BETWEEN
YOU & ME

BETWEEN
YOU & ME

Confessions of a Comma Queen

MARY NORRIS

W. W. NORTON & COMPANY

New York • *London*

For information about permission to reproduce selections from this book,
write to Permissions, W. W. Norton & Company, Inc.,
500 Fifth Avenue, New York, NY 10110

For information about special discounts for bulk purchases, please
contact W. W. Norton Special Sales at specialsales@wwnorton.com or
800-233-4830

Manufacturing by Courier Westford
Book design by Ellen Cipriano
Production manager: Louise Parasmo

Library of Congress Cataloging-in-Publication Data

Norris, Mary (Editor)
Between you & me : confessions of a Comma Queen / Mary Norris. —
First Edition.
pages cm
Includes bibliographical references and index.
ISBN 978-0-393-24018-4 (hardcover)
1. English language—Punctuation. 2. Comma. 3. English language—
Errors in usage. I. Title. II. Title: Between you and me.
PE1450.N67 2015
428.2—dc23

2014043252

W. W. Norton & Company, Inc.
500 Fifth Avenue, New York, N.Y. 10110
www.wwnorton.com

W. W. Norton & Company Ltd.
Castle House, 75/76 Wells Street, London W1T 3QT

1 2 3 4 5 6 7 8 9 0

For you and you
and you.

CONTENTS

Of course, when you correct the errors of others,
do so with kindness, in the hope that later writers
will be as kind when they correct yours.

—Francis A. Burkle-Young and Saundra Rose Maley,
The Art of the Footnote

BETWEEN
YOU & ME

CONFESSION OF A COMMA QUEEN

L ET'S GET ONE THING STRAIGHT right from the beginning: I didn't set out to be a comma queen. The first job I ever had, the summer I was fifteen, was checking feet at a public pool in Cleveland. I was a "key girl"—"Key personnel" was the job title on my pay stub (I made seventy-five dollars a week). I never knew what that was supposed to mean. I was not in charge of any keys, and my position was by no means crucial to the operation of the pool, although I did clean the bathrooms.

Everyone had to follow an elaborate ritual before getting into the pool: tuck your hair into a hideous bathing cap (if you were a girl), shower, wade through a footbath spiked with disinfectant that tinted your feet orange, and stand in line to have your toes checked. This took place at a special wooden bench, like those things that shoe salesmen use, except that instead of a miniature sliding board and a size stick for the customer's foot it had a stick with a foot-shaped platform on top. The prospective swimmer put one foot at a time on the platform and, leaning forward, used his fingers to spread out his toes so that the foot checker could make sure he didn't have athlete's foot. Only then could he pass into the pool. I have never heard of foot checkers in any city besides Cleveland, where their presence was taken for granted, and can only speculate that at one time there was an outbreak of athlete's foot on the shores of Lake Erie, and a crusading public health official, determined to stamp it out, had these benches knocked together and hired people to sit at them, checking feet.

I am not particularly nostalgic about my foot-checking days. Nor do I wish to revisit my time at the Cleveland Costume Company, where I worked after graduation. I had gone to Douglass College, the women's college of Rutgers University, in New Brunswick, New Jersey, and I had returned ignominiously to the nest because I couldn't think of anything better to do. The costume company was fun for a while: renting props to local TV shows, putting together costumes for summer-stock productions of Restoration drama. On my first day, a young black woman, Yvonne, was setting Santa beards in rollers so that they would be curly by Christmas. An older black woman worked in the kitchen, starching and ironing the clown ruffs and nuns' wimples. She changed from street shoes into bedroom slippers when she got to work, and said things like "My dogs is killin' me." The boss was Mrs. Pizzino ("*P* as in Peter, *I*, double *Z* as in zebra, *I*, *N*, *O*," she would say, spelling her last name out over the phone), and under her tutelage I learned to repair big papier-mâché animal heads and not to paint the panther's eyes blue.

Halloween had always been my favorite holiday, and I borrowed a costume from work—a hooded green corduroy robe like something a fairy-tale dwarf would wear—and threw a party in my parents' basement. It featured copious amounts of alcohol and candy. One of the guests came as a penis; another as a Ku Klux Klansman. Initially, I was sorry that Yvonne declined my invitation, but not anymore. When the party was over, I decided that my career at the costume company had peaked and I was going to quit. Accordingly, I slept in the next day, and was awakened by my mother, saying that Mrs. Badina was on the phone. (Mom never got Mrs. Pizzino's name straight.) I explained to my boss that now that Halloween was over I thought I'd quit. Her response was "Get in here." There is just as much to do at a costume company after the holiday as there is in the weeks leading up to it. I stuck it out through the Christmas season, and, after all the Santa suits had been cleaned and put away and Yvonne was rolling up the beards again, I started looking around.

I called a local dairy and asked whether there were any openings for milkmen. I had had a fantasy for years about owning a dairy farm. I liked cows: they led a placid yet productive life. I'd gone to Rutgers partly because it had a renowned department of dairy science. I'd taken one mini-course in how to judge dairy cattle and learned the differences between Holsteins, Guernseys, Jerseys, and Brown Swiss cows. "We've never had a lady drive a milk truck, but there's no reason not," a man said, and he agreed to let me come in and talk. The plant was all gleaming stainless steel, heated milk undercut with a bracing whiff of ammonia. It was the first time I could be completely honest in a job interview. I didn't have any experience, but I was sincerely interested in the dairy industry.

On a frigid morning in February, I went along with a

milkman on a route in Fairview, a suburb west of Cleveland. The milk truck had two sets of pedals, one with the standard three for a stick shift, for driving sitting down when you were going long distances, and the other for driving standing up, when you were hopping between houses. This second set had just two pedals: the clutch and the brake were combined in one. When you needed to slow down or shift gears, your left foot squeezed down through the clutch to the brake on one pedal, and you had to lift your right foot off the accelerator and balance on one heel.

The route was available, and they gave me the job. A generous friend lent me her car for a crash course in how to drive a stick shift. The foreman who was training me noticed that I handled the truck better standing up than sitting down. The seat was designed to fold up and swing around to the side, where it could be stowed out of the way. All that folding and swinging had loosened it up, so when I turned the steering wheel the seat swung in the opposite direction, and I would find myself facing out the side instead of in the direction the truck was going, as if I were on some disorienting amusement-park ride. At the foreman's suggestion, I was driving back to the plant standing up, on Brookpark Road, out near the airport. I went through an underpass, on the far side of which was a traffic light, and I was almost under it when I saw that it was red, so I had to slam on the brake and try to steer while gripping the steering wheel and balancing on one heel, and I lost control. The truck crashed into a concrete barrier. The foreman was thrown into the ice-cream freezer, and I landed on the floor. He was OK. I was bruised and humiliated. The plant had its own tow truck and mechanic, and I rode back with the mechanic, wanting to bum one of his unfiltered Camels. The foreman got blamed, because the boss said he shouldn't have had me driving standing up, and I got another chance.

I had some really nice customers—there was a couple who bought only a pint of half-and-half once a week for their coffee—and I had some deadbeats, the kind of people who knew that if they ever paid their bill in full you'd drop them. There was a man who rehabilitated coin changers, those contraptions with barrels for quarters, nickels, pennies, and dimes; we wore them on our belts. The houses had milk chutes, or boxes beside the door, or you put the milk between the storm door and the inside door, and shouted "Milkman!" I wasn't a man, but I didn't like the word "lady"—it seemed not feminist—so I wouldn't holler "Milklady!" and "milkmaid" was a little too fanciful. I settled for "milkwoman," which was a bit too anatomically correct and made me sound like a wet nurse. I muffled the last syllables.

I had half a mind to stay in Cleveland and try to marry the boss's son (he raised beef cattle), but I gave up the milk route to accept a fellowship at the University of Vermont, where I had applied, too late, the year before. While pursuing a master's degree in English, I kept up my interest in the dairy industry— UVM had an agricultural school and a famous ice-cream program. I even learned to milk cows, though they were university cows (Holsteins—big producers). My first job once the academic life had worn me down was packaging mozzarella on the night shift in a cheese factory. A team of women, wearing white rubber aprons, yellow rubber gloves, green rubber boots, and hairnets, pulled bricks of mozzarella out of vats of cold salt water, labeled them, bagged them, sealed the bags, boxed the cheese, and stacked the boxes. I had a secret yen to operate the forklift truck. The Popeye-style muscles I developed in my forearms atrophied soon after I moved to New York. Sometimes, on the sides of trucks making deliveries to pizzerias, I still recognize the logos of cheese wholesalers—Vesuvio, Cremona, in red, white, and green—whose labels we slapped onto loaves of mozzarella in Vermont. I don't suppose that I will ever belong to the Brotherhood of Teamsters again (though I maintain my chauffeur's license) or have calluses on my palms from handling a stainless-steel carrier full of half-gallon milk cartons.

I started reading *The New Yorker* in graduate school in Vermont. I sometimes visited my brother in New York. He had gone to the Art Students League, where he made friends with a woman in his portrait class named Jeanne Fleischmann. She was married to Peter Fleischmann, the chairman of the board of *The New Yorker.* His father, Raoul Fleischmann, had been the co-founder of the magazine, with Harold Ross. On one visit, I picked up a copy of the magazine. It was dated February 24, 1975. Eustace Tilley was on the cover, and the contents included a piece by E. B. White: Letter from the East. It was the anniversary issue—*The New Yorker*'s fiftieth anniversary.

Eventually, I met the Fleischmanns. I was doing research for my master's thesis, on James Thurber, and while Peter was away on business he let me sit in his office and look through bound volumes of the magazine. At the Morgan Library, in an exhibit of books that had belonged to writers, I found a grammar mistake on the wall label accompanying Thurber's copy of Hemingway's *Green Hills of Africa*, in which he had made pencil drawings of Papa and Memsahib on safari. I was given permission to examine the book. (I made freehand copies of the illustrations and appended them to my thesis. My examiners were not amused.) In Vermont, I kept two stacks of magazines on my lobster-crate coffee table, one of *Hoard's Dairyman* and one of *The New Yorker.*

It was the summer of 1977, and there were some wonderful things in *The New Yorker:* Woody Allen's story "The Kugelmass Episode" (it was also the year of *Annie Hall*), charming pieces by Calvin Trillin with illustrations by Edward Koren, John McPhee's series about Alaska, "Coming into the Country." I had never read McPhee before, and I was dumbstruck, as much by the sweep of his subject matter—Alaska—as by his precise, loving placement of words. He describes the view from the window of Jim Scott, his neighbor and landlord, in Eagle, Alaska:

> In the view's right-middle ground is Eagle Creek, where he and I once fished for grayling. It is in the United States, and if it is not God's country, God should try to get it, a place so beautiful it beggars description—a clear, fast stream, which on that day was still covered on both sides and almost to the center with two or three feet of white and blue ice. The steep knobby hills above were pale green with new aspen leaves; there were occasional white birch, dark interspersed cones of isolate spruce, here and again patches of tundra. Overhead was a flotilla of gray-hulled, white-sailed clouds. Fresh snow was on the mountains in the distance. The Scotts have all that framed in their Thermopane—a window that could have been lifted from a wall in Paramus and driven here, to the end of the end of the road. The window is synecdoche, is Eagle itself—a lens, a monocular, framing the wild, holding

the vision that draws people up the long trail to the edge of things to have a look and see.

Synecdoche: what was that? The context defined it for me—a small thing writ large—but I looked it up anyway. It's from the Greek *syn* (with) + *ekdoche* (sense, interpretation), from *ekdechesthai*, to receive, understand; "to receive jointly": "a figure of speech by which a part is put for the whole (as *fifty sail* for *fifty ships*), the whole for a part (as *society* for *high society*), the species for the genus (as *cutthroat* for *assassin*), the genus for the species (as *a creature* for *a man*), or the name of the material for the thing made (as *boards* for *stage*)." It has four syllables, with the accent on the second syllable: "sin-NECK-duh-kee." A near rhyme with Schenectady.

I cannot explain the effect this word had on me, except to say that it made me ecstatic. I was like that cartoon dog who, when given a biscuit, hugs himself and levitates. In addition to what the word was describing—the wilds of Alaska—it was a window onto the writing itself. When McPhee uses an unfamiliar word, you can be sure that it's the only word for what he's trying to say, and he savors it, he rolls the syllables in his mouth as if words were food and he were licking his chops.

I made up my mind to move to New York in the fall of 1977. I drove there in my 1965 Plymouth Fury II, with my cat, my books pared down to the bare essentials, and two hundred dollars. The Fleischmanns, whose grown children had moved out, were still in parental mode, and they befriended me readily. I spent many a cocktail hour in their den, drinking their Heineken and listening to Peter's stories. Peter drank Scotch-and-water, chain-smoked, and swallowed Maalox by the handful. He told war stories (he was in the Battle of the Bulge) and stories about Yale and about his father, Raoul (the family came from Vienna), and croquet games with Harpo Marx banking a shot off a spare tire that he had sawed apart and wrapped around a tree trunk.

That fall, I had a reverse commute from the financial district to Paterson, New Jersey, where I was washing dishes in a friend's restaurant. The friend paid my bus fare and gave me all the beer I could drink. In return, I tried not to throw away the silverware when I scraped the dishes. Often I got off the bus and walked over the George Washington Bridge on the way home. I worked on my thesis, and sometimes despaired. Peter pointed out that even if I never finished the thesis or got the master's degree, it was no reason to despair. Peter had no influence in the editorial department—like his father, he kept business and editorial strictly separate. But he offered to call Bob Bingham, the executive editor, and ask him to talk with me. We met on the Friday after Thanksgiving. Bingham was very nice, but there were no openings.

I quit the dishwashing job and worked as a cashier at Korvettes during the Christmas rush. I could not figure out whether to be sad or relieved when the management did not recognize my talent and keep me on. I did temp work, first at an insurance company in the financial district. It was about a block from the loft I lived in on John Street, and my commute consisted of going down one elevator and up another. A handsome man with coppery hair posed at the Xerox machine. I moved on to a temp job as a statistical typist at a bank in Midtown, filling in interest amounts on tax forms. I was on the verge of trying to get a hack license so that I could drive a cab when Peter, possibly sensing an ambulance in my future, suggested that I give Bingham a follow-up call.

There was an opening! Two, in fact, one in the typing pool and one in the editorial library. I flunked the test for the typing pool. It was on an electric typewriter, and I was used to a manual—at least, that was my excuse. If my hands trembled over the keyboard, the typewriter took off without me. The interview in the editorial library was like the one at the dairy in that I didn't have to lie to get the job. I wanted to work at *The New Yorker*, and once I got a whiff of the library—that bookish, dusty, paste-and-paper smell so peculiar to libraries—I felt that I was in my element. Helen Stark, who was only the second person ever to be in charge of the library, had a noble head—you could see her profile on a coin—and strong features. She and three girls sat at desks that faced each other in a cloverleaf arrangement. Helen gave me a typing test—on a manual typewriter, cramming words onto an index card (I aced it)—and borrowed an empty office for the interview. I remember her arranging her skirt, which was black and wide at the hem, when she crossed her legs. (My own skirt was a forest-green Danskin wraparound that a friend had picked up at a thrift shop in New Jersey, and I didn't realize until the next time I wore it that one end of the hem hung some eight inches longer than the other.) I was all aglow, and Helen warned me that it was not a glamorous job. But she knew from experience that nothing she said could dim my enthusiasm, or overturn my conviction that I would soon be one of the "young friends" whose "letters" were published in Talk of the Town. After the interview, Jeanne Fleischmann took me to lunch at the Algonquin and then to the Russian Tea Room, where I ordered a cup of Russian tea. I was too superstitious to celebrate prematurely.

The call came the next day, a Friday, and I started on Monday. It was snowing, and Helen Stark took me upstairs to the makeup department, on the nineteenth floor. The magazine went to press on Monday afternoon, and the men in makeup, who lived in the Bronx, had come in on the train the night before and stayed in a hotel across the street so that the blizzard wouldn't prevent them from getting to work. Their job was to do the page layout, fitting columns and cartoons and counting picas. A notice from the editor, William Shawn, went up on the bulletin board, saying that anyone whose work was not "essential" could go home. Nobody wanted to think they were not essential.

Joe Carroll was the head of makeup. He pulled out a chair for Helen and made us coffee. Johnny Murphy, second-in-command, was the joker of the crew. He carried a briefcase with his lunch in it. Bernie McAteer was small and wiry, a bachelor, mostly bald. Bill Fitzgerald looked like Walter Matthau. There were two apprentices, both Irish, John and Pat, and a messenger named Carmine. It was cozy in the makeup room during the blizzard. They reminisced about the blackout of '77, just the summer before, when an editor named Gardner Botsford had marshaled everyone into the makeup department and organized the evacuation. It was February 6, 1978. I remember because the next day was my birthday. It was still snowing, and the office was closed again. At lunchtime, I tromped up Fifth Avenue to Scribner's and bought myself a book I wanted: *Caught in the Web of Words*, a biography of James Murray, the first editor of the *OED*.

As Helen and I were leaving that night, an editor named Pat Crow got on the elevator at the eighteenth floor with us. I noticed his boots—big mud-green rubber boots—and said, "Those are the kind of boots we wore in the cheese factory." He looked at Helen and said, "So this is the next stop after the cheese factory?"

When I came up out of the subway at the City Hall station,

intending to stop at the store and buy myself a cake and some ice cream (I was going to skip the candles), fireworks were drifting over the snow at One Police Plaza, muffled but dazzling. It was Chinese New Year, the Year of the Horse. It felt like a good omen: soft fireworks for an entry-level position at *The New Yorker.*

———

That was more than thirty-five years ago. And it has now been more than twenty years since I became a page OK'er—a position that exists only at *The New Yorker,* where you query-proofread pieces and manage them, with the editor, the author, a fact checker, and a second proofreader, until they go to press. An editor once called us prose goddesses; another job description might be comma queen. Except for writing, I have never seriously considered doing anything else.

One of the things I like about my job is that it draws on the entire person: not just your knowledge of grammar and punctuation and usage and foreign languages and literature but also your experience of travel, gardening, shipping, singing, plumbing, Catholicism, midwesternism, mozzarella, the A train, New Jersey. And in turn it feeds you more experience. In the hierarchy of prose goddesses, I am way, way down the list. But what expertise I have acquired I want to pass along.

My fondest hope is that just from looking at the title you will learn to say fearlessly "between you and me" (not "I"), whether or not you actually buy the book and penetrate to the innards of the objective case. Nobody knows everything—one of the pleasures of language is that there is always something new to learn— and everybody makes mistakes. Regularly, my grasp of the subjunctive slips, and I need to visit the grammatical equivalent of a chiropractor. On my way out of the house one morning, I grabbed a usage manual to read in the car while I waited for the street cleaner to go by, in the street ballet called alternate side of the street parking, during which New Yorkers who own cars but are too cheap to park them in lots or garages compete for a legal spot. "The subjunctive sounds scarier than it is and has a tendency to fill people with horror," I read. Uh-oh.

You use the subjunctive mood when something is contrary to fact. A classic example is "If I were a rich man." The subjunctive almost always follows "as if" ("She looked as if she were frozen behind the wheel") and may also be used in wishes: "I wish I were home in bed." Where I get twisted up is when there's a negative involved, as in "If it were not for these stupid street-cleaning rules, I would be home in bed." Does the negative cancel out the contrary-to-factness? It does not. There *are* those stupid street-cleaning rules.

Just then a woman rapped on my car window and said, incredulously, "Miss, are you studying grammar?" (She had a strong New York accent, so it came out more like "Miss, you studyin' grandma?") I nodded. "My grammar is terrible," she said. "Is that a good book?" Yes, I said, and showed her the cover: *My Grammar and I . . . Or Should That Be Me?*, by Caroline Taggart and J. A. Wines. It was published in the States by Reader's Digest, and is easy to read and digest.

The woman read off the title and the authors' names to fix them in her memory, thanked me, and went on her way. Only then did I notice that it was ten o'clock: the street cleaner had never come, and all the other parkers had gradually slithered across the street and taken spots and were locking their cars and leaving. Every spot on the block was taken. I was going to have to pay to park my car in a lot. Driving away, I felt happier than I'd have thought possible after being skunked out of a parking spot, and it was because of that woman, because she was interested in grammar. I wished I had given her my copy of the book. But I didn't. So this is for her and for all of you who want to feel better about your grammar.

Chapter 1

SPELLING IS FOR WEIRDOS

"WEIRD" HAS LONG BEEN ONE of my favorite words, and I'm sure I overuse it. It is one of those words which defy the old "*i* before *e* except after *c*" rule (a rule that applies mostly to words derived from the Latin; I always have to pause before spelling "siege" and "seize" and "niece"). Educated people—friends of mine—have been known to misspell it as "wierd." I had a traumatic experience with the word in fourth grade. I had completed an assignment for history, which that year was devoted to Ohio. I had attempted to liven it up, at least for me, by writing about eccentrics associated with Ohio. I remember two of them: Johnny Appleseed and Annie Oakley. I titled the project "Weirdos" and printed the word diagonally in capital letters, spacing them out carefully on the cover of the clip binder, starting in the upper left-hand corner. I was so determined to get the *ei* right that only later did I notice I had left out the *r*, committing an unsightly handmade typo: "WEIDOS."

Why should we care about spelling? What is it about orthography—its Greek roots mean "straight scratching"—that ennobles our enterprise? Why should we try to master spelling, especially now, when we have machines to do it for us? Back in the twentieth century, we thought that robots would have taken over by this time, and, in a way, they have. But robots as a race have proved disappointing. Instead of getting to boss around underlings made of steel and plastic with circuitry and blinking lights and tank treads, like Rosie the maid on *The Jetsons*, we humans have outfitted ourselves with robotic external organs. Our iPods dictate what we listen to next, gadgets in our cars tell us which way to go, and smartphones finish our sentences for us. We have become our own robots.

Some people might wonder why we still need copy editors when we have spell-check. Although it is a pain whenever I want to double a consonant before a suffix, per *New Yorker* style, and the spell-check prefers the no-frills version—"mislabeled," say, instead of "mislabelled"—and I have to go back and poke in the extra letter and then put up with a disapproving red line under the word, I would never disable spell-check. That would be hubris. Autocorrect I could do without. It thinks I am stupid and clumsy, and while it's true that I don't know how to disable it and I can't text with my thumbs like a teenager (though I am prehensile), why would I let a machine tell me what I want to say? I text someone "Good night" in German, and instead of "Gute Nacht" I send "Cute Nachos." I type "adverbial," and it comes out "adrenal," which is like a knife thrust to my adverbial gland. Invited to dinner, I text my friend to ask whether I can bring anything, and she replies that the "food and dissertation" are under control. Good news, I guess. I understand to bring wine and not ask anyone the topic of his PhD thesis.

At work, I try to remember to run a spell-check on every piece at some point. It does catch typos. But the reason that the spell-checker will never replace the copy editor is that it doesn't recognize context and therefore cannot distinguish between homophones, words that sound alike but are spelled differently and have different meanings: "peddle" (to sell) and "pedal" (to push with the feet), "horde" (crowd) and "hoard" (stash, treasure), "rye" (bread or whiskey) and "wry" (manner), "tale" (story) and "tail" (posterior appendage), "cannon" (the weapon) and "canon" (the received wisdom), "lead" (the heavy metal) and "led" (past tense of "lead"), let alone "roomy," "roomie," "rheumy," and "Rumi."

The English language is full of words that are just waiting to be misspelled, and the world is full of sticklers, ready to pounce. Ours is not a phonetic language, like Italian and Spanish and Modern Greek, where certain letters and combinations of letters can be relied on to produce consistent sounds. English has many silent letters. And its motley origins make it fiendishly difficult to untangle. Besides the Germanic roots of our Anglo-Saxon tongue and the influence of Latin (Emperor Hadrian) and French (the Norman invasion), and borrowings from Greek and Italian and Portuguese and even a soupçon of Basque, American English has a lot of Dutch from early settlers in the East; plenty of Spanish, from the conquistadores and missionaries who explored the West; and a huge vocabulary of place-names from Native American languages, often blended with French, for added confusion. As Noah Webster, the stickler-in-chief, pointed out way back in 1783, "Several of our vowels have four or five different sounds; another four sounds are often expressed by five, six or seven different characters. The case is much the same with our consonants."

A good dictionary can only help. At *The New Yorker*, we use *Webster's*—in fact, we use three editions of *Webster's*, following a sort of sacred hierarchy. When I look up a word in the line of duty—after first consulting our style book (a venerable legal-size three-ring binder, its pages encased in plastic sleeves) to make sure that the founders haven't prescribed a peculiar spelling—I turn to *Merriam-Webster's Collegiate Dictionary*, now in its eleventh edition. We call it the Little Red Web. (When Eleven came out in 2003, all the Tens were retired. We tried to find good homes for them—you don't just throw a dictionary away! I reserved a few and recycled them as gifts.) Merriam-Webster constantly updates its basic desk dictionary. Every home should have a Little Red Web, the way a hotel room has a Gideon Bible.

If we cannot find something in the Little Red Web, our next resort is *Webster's New International Dictionary (Unabridged), Second Edition*, which we call Web II. First published in 1934, it was the Great American Dictionary and is still an object of desire: 3,194 pages long, with leisurely definitions and detailed illustrations. It was supplanted in 1961 by *Webster's Third*, whose editors, led by Philip Gove, caused a huge ruckus in the dictionary world by including commonly used words without warning people about which ones would betray their vulgar origins. On the publication of this dictionary, which we call Web 3, a seismic shift occurred between prescriptivists (who tell you what to do) and descriptivists (who describe what people say, without judging it). In March of 1962, *The New Yorker*, a bastion of prescriptivism, published an essay by Dwight Macdonald that attacked the dictionary and its linguistic principles: "The objection is not to recording the facts of actual usage. It is to failing to give the information that would enable the reader to decide which usage he wants to adopt." "Transpire" and "enthuse" are still disapproved of. Since the great dictionary war of the early sixties, there has been an institutional distrust of Web 3. It's good for some scientific terms, we say, patronizingly. Its look is a lot cleaner than that of Web II. Lexicology aside, it is just not as beautiful. I would not haul a Web 3 home. You can even tell by the way it is abbreviated in our offices that it is less distinguished: *Webster's Second* gets the Roman numeral, as if it were royalty, but *Webster's Third* must make do with a plain old Arabic numeral.

Some people around the office use the online *Webster's*. Nothing wrong with that. The dictionary has come with a disk for years now and has been free online since 1996 (though you have to put up with ads). I've never gotten into the habit of looking up words online. I like paper and the opportunities for browsing, and have not been able to bring myself to give it up just yet.

In our hierarchy of dictionaries, if we have exhausted Web II and Web 3, we turn to the *Random House Unabridged Dictionary* (second edition), which came out in 1987. Its first edition, of 1966, exploited the war over Webs II and 3 by offering a fresh voice, free of conflict. I have a weakness for the *Random House*, and sometimes, if a word seems recent, I will go straight to *RH* rather than dabble in Web II or 3. I like it because it includes a lot of proper names, both historical and fictional, as if to thumb its nose at the makers of Scrabble.

The New Yorker is so deeply invested in *Webster's*, trusting implic-
itly in the American brand name, even to the exclusion of the
Oxford dictionaries (the *OED* may be endlessly fascinating, but
it is not a practical reference book), that I began to wonder just
who this Noah Webster was, anyway. Biographies make him out
to be "the forgotten founding father," but as a lexicographer he
gets nowhere near the respect that Samuel Johnson got. And yet
Webster's accomplishment was monumental. The habits of generations of Americans—writers, editors, academics—descend from
him. At his birthplace, a farmhouse (now a sleepy little museum)
in West Hartford, Connecticut, I bought a facsimile edition of
a small book he compiled in 1783, *A Grammatical Institute of the
English Language*, which became known as the Blue-Back Speller.
Webster had attended Yale during the Revolutionary War (class
of 1778), hoping to be a lawyer, but instead he became a school-
teacher. He was so appalled at his students' pronunciation and
spelling that he put together the speller, afire to lift the standards
of his compatriots while simultaneously rebelling against England by beginning to standardize an American language. Noah
Webster turned out to be a marketing genius, peddling the Blue-
Back Speller—the seed of the Little Red Web—all up and down
the East Coast, and ultimately compiling a two-volume *American
Dictionary of the English Language*.

The first thing you notice about the speller is that it employs
on its cover the archaic long *s*, which looks like an *f*. The whole
book is like that, and if you stop fooling around and just pronounce the *f*'s as *s*'s, as intended, Noah Webster turns out to be
lucid and eloquent, but if you pronounce them as *f*'s you cannot

take Webfter ferioufly at all. It is as if the book had been written by fomeone with a profound fpeech defect. The Blue-Back
is about four by six inches and 119 pages long. Webster always
intended to call it a speller, but early on he was swayed by the
president of Yale, Ezra Stiles, who liked a title modeled on a Cal-
vinist tract, and Webster, hoping for his endorsement, complied
with "Inftitute." It says on the cover that the book is "Defigned
for the ufe of Englifh Schools" and quotes a line of Latin—"Ufus
eft Norma Loquendi"—attributing it to Cicero. The biographies
translate "Usus est Norma Loquendi" variously as "General custom is the rule of speaking" and "Usage should determine the
rule of speech." In other words, "Usage rules." Noah Webster was
a descriptivist!

Though Webster was, in the words of James Murray, a "born
definer," he was not always reliable as a scholar. For instance,
the quotation he attributes to Cicero is actually from Horace, a
passage in *Ars Poetica* about the balance between neologism and
conservative usage and the coinage of words:

> *Multa renascentur quae iam cecidere, cadentque*
> *Quae nunc sunt in honore uocabula, si uolet usus,*
> *Quem penes arbitrium est et ius et norma loquendi.*

A friend looked it up for me and provided a literal translation:

> Many vocabulary words will be born which now have
>   perished, and will fall
> Vocabulary which is now in honor, if usage should wish,
> Under whom rests judgment and the law and the norm
>   of speaking.

Norma Loquendi is a joke among English-language pundits: she is the goddess of proper usage.

The Blue-Back is organized into tables of sounds and words, of graduated difficulty, starting with "Words of three or four letters" and moving on to "Easy words of two syllables, accented on the first" and finally getting to "Words of five syllables accented on the fourth ("im a gin a tion . . . qual i fi ca tion . . . re gen e ra tion"). It is tempting to view Webster's lists as free association ("bed, fed, led, red, wed") offering a window into his soul ("glut, shut, smut, slut"); he was a bachelor at the time ("La dy, la zy, le gal, li ar, like ly, li ning, li on, lone ly"). He italicized the silent letters and the letter *s* when it is pronounced as a *z* (in fact, he suggests that when *s* is voiced it be called *ez*). He wanted to rename certain letters of the alphabet: *h* (aitch) should be "more properly" "he"; *w* (double-u) should be "we"; *y* (why) should be "yi." Yikes. It is owing to Webster that in America the British "zed" became "zee."

"Spelling is the art of dividing words into their proper syllables in order to find their true pronunciation," he writes. The tone of his instructions to the teacher is often ill-tempered, as if he expected opposition. "To attack deep rooted prejudices and oppose the current of opinion, is a task of great difficulty and hazard," he writes, summarizing the murderous thoughts of thwarted, self-righteous copy editors: "Even errour becomes too sacred to be violated by the assaults of innovation." He fulminates in the introduction: "The sound of the half-vowels is obvious in the words *feeble, baptism, heaven*. . . . Some people, finding a little difficulty in pronouncing the half-vowels, give the full sound of *e* before them, thus *feebel, heaven*, &c. which is an errour that ought to be corrected in infancy." His footnotes, too, are passionate. He puts an asterisk next to "mercy," "perfect," and "person," and rails, "These words are vulgarly pronounced *marcy, parfect, parson,* &c. This is a vicious habit, contracted by carelessness, which destroys the beauty of pronunciation by giving the vowel wrong sound and wrong quantity. It is an errour universal among inaccurate speakers to sound *e* before *r* like *a*; I therefore request, once for all, that it may be attended to."

Considering that the Blue-Back was aimed at schoolchildren, I wasn't expecting to learn much from it. I noted what words got Webster's goat when his students mispronounced them (children in colonial times made some of the same mistakes kids make today: "punkin" for "pumpkin" and "chimbley" for "chimney"). But as I paged through the book, I gradually compiled a long list of words that I'd been mispronouncing all my life, at least mentally—many of them I'd never had the occasion or the nerve to pronounce out loud. For instance, nobody says "huzza" anymore, so how was I to know that it has its accent on the last syllable, like "hurrah"? "Uxorious," meaning "excessively attentive to one's wife," has a soft *u*; it's not "you-xorious." (I once asked a married man if there was a word for a woman who was excessively attentive to her husband, and he said, "Yes: wonderful.") And "elegiac" is pronounced "e-LEE-gi-ac"? I've always said "el-e-JIE-ac," and would look askance at anyone who pronounced it "e-LEE-gi-ac," except as a joke. "Chimaera" begins with a "k" sound (it's Greek) and takes its accent on the second syllable: "chi-MAE-ra." I always thought it was "shimmera"— accent on the first syllable, a pronunciation that may be wrong but is more evocative of the word's meaning: something illusory and a bit monstrous.

Before encountering the Blue-Back, I thought I had reached

the bottom of the well of mispronunciation. I had learned the three *D*'s: "desultory" ("DEZ-ul-to-ry"; I always think it's "de-ZUL-to-ry"), "disheveled" ("di-SHEV-eld," not "dis-HEAV-eld"), and "detritus" ("de-TRY-tus," not "DET-ri-tus"). Now every day I hear a new one. On *The Simpsons*, Lisa remarks on Homer's rationale for stealing cable TV: "Dad, that sounds spurious." ("Thank you, Lisa," he replies.) The *u* has the *y* sound, as in "curious." I'd been pronouncing it as if it meant "of or relating to spurs." As long as I was looking up the pronunciation of "spurious," I read the definition and etymology: it means "false" and is from the Latin for "bastard." Thank you, Lisa.

One thing I will say for *Webster's* online dictionary: many words come not just with a phonetic rendering of the pronunciation but with an icon that you can click on to hear someone pronounce the word for you. This could have saved me countless instances of embarrassment when I have laughed out loud at someone who was pronouncing something correctly.

From his start with the speller and his sputtering law practice, Webster went on to edit New York City's first daily newspaper, the *American Minerva*, expressly at the behest of George Washington. When Webster retired from the newspaper business, he moved back to Connecticut—to New Haven, where he bought the Benedict Arnold House (it was going cheap)—and turned to compiling an American dictionary. Benjamin Franklin, who was already in his eighties when he befriended Webster, and who advocated spelling reform, had encouraged the younger man to adopt his ideas. Franklin proposed that we lose *c, w, y,* and *j;*

modify *a* and *u* to represent their different sounds; and adopt a
new form of *s* for *sh* and a variation on *y* for *ng* as well as tweak
the *h* of *th* to distinguish the sounds of "thy" and "thigh," "swath"
and "swathe." If Franklin had had his way, he would have been
the Saint Cyril of America—Cyril "perfected" the Greek alphabet for the Russian language; hence the Cyrillic alphabet—and
American English would look like Turkish.

Webster went along with him to an extent, but Franklin had
brought to America the standard grammar text for students—
Dilworth's New Guide to the English Tongue—buying the rights
and profiting from sales, and it was *Dilworth's* that Webster was
hoping to supersede. Early on, he was an advocate of dropping
silent letters. One of his books was titled *A Collection of Essays and
Fugitiv Writings.* Traditionalists have always been against this
kind of simplification, on the ground that there is so much history
in spelling: clues to a word's etymology, its radical meaning in
Latin or Greek, German or Basque or Anglo-Saxon. Before the
two-volume dictionary that was the capstone of Webster's career,
he put out a *Compendious* dictionary, in 1806, in which he experimented with phonetic spellings. *Compendious* sounds heavy,
ponderous, but the dictionary defines it as "concise and compre-
hensive." The *Compendious* gave brief definitions of 37,000 words
in a single volume, with no etymologies or citations of usage.
(For instance, "skunk: a quadruped remarkable for its smell.")
On the title page Webster wrote, "The ORTHOGRAPHY is, in
some instances, corrected." Some of his innovations caught on:
the British "gaol" in America became "jail," thank God. (I still
can't look at Oscar Wilde's "The Ballad of Reading Gaol" without thinking that it has something unpleasant to do with gall
and reading—not that I am suggesting we change it to Redding

Jail.) He took the *u* out of "mould." (Now, there's an epitaph!) But many of Webster's attempts to make the orthography match the pronunciation were not popular. One of his biographers, Harlow Giles Unger, writes, "Americans rejected *ake* for *ache*, *hainous* for *heinous*, *soop* for *soup*, *cloke* for *cloak*, and *spunge* for *sponge*. Efforts to eliminate silent letters had similarly mixed results. . . . [T]he public refused to adopt *ax*, *imagin*, *medicin*, *doctrin*, or *wo*, and Webster restored the final *e*'s in his subsequent dictionaries." He also failed to persuade his countrymen that "tung" was an improvement over "tongue."

In the end, Webster's spelling reforms seem conservative. He eliminated the *u* in the British spelling of such words as "colour" and "flavour." He took the *k* off the end of words like "musick" and "traffick," rejecting a spelling preferred by Samuel Johnson. (Johnson was a hero of Webster's, and he did copy from Johnson—why reinvent the wheel?—but he left out the dirty bits.) He changed *c* to *s* in "defense" and "offense," and transposed the *re* into *er* in such words as "theater" and "center." Other reforms came from the people, who were already spelling words like "masque" and "risque" and "racquet" with a *k* instead of a *qu*.

Before writing the dictionary, Webster spent an entire decade kneading the language. He had a semicircular desk with two dozen dictionaries and had studied twenty-six languages— Latin, Greek, French, German, Danish, Icelandic, Finnish, Norwegian, Arabic, Hebrew, and Sanskrit among them—and he would turn from one dictionary to another, tracing the words back to a common source in what he called Chaldee, the universal language spoken before the time of the Tower of Babel. (Webster was a born-again Christian, enamored of biblical truth.) The idea of consulting etymology in order to arrive at a word's authentic spelling is a sound one. The trouble was that Webster was making it up.

"Etymology" is from the Greek and means the study (*logia*) of the "literal meaning of a word according to its origin" (*etymon*). (Not to be confused with "entomology," the study of insects [*entomon*].) It can be a huge help in spelling. For instance, people sometimes misspell "iridescent." It's a trick word that often appears on copy-editing tests. *Webster's Collegiate* supplies this enthusiastic definition for "iridescence": "a lustrous rainbowlike play of color caused by differential refraction of light waves (as from an oil slick, soap bubble, or fish scales) that tends to change as the angle of view changes." Rather than just try to memorize the spelling, if you look at the etymology—study the entrails of the word—you find that "iris, irid" is a combining form that comes from the Greek Iris, the goddess of the rainbow and the messenger of the gods. Wow! Like Webster, I could go off the deep end in finding significance in this: it seems like magic—a word that appeared in Homer's *Iliad* and that we associate with Noah's ark (the rainbow), and with optimism and promise, connects with puddles in Cleveland that I marveled at as a girl (there was a lot of grease in the puddles in Cleveland) and an indelible image from the opening pages of *The Catcher in the Rye*, in which Salinger has Holden remark on the "gasoline rainbow." Anyway, once you know that "iridescent" comes from Iris, you'll never spell it wrong.

———

Webster finished the dictionary in England—he was such an outcast that he actually thought he'd have better luck publishing it over there. Webster's two-volume *American Dictionary of the English Language* was published in New Haven in 1828. He died on May 28, 1843—he had followed up on the dictionary by translating the Bible—and is buried next to Eli Whitney, in the Grove Street Cemetery, near the Yale campus, in New Haven. I have visited the cemetery, walked through its monumental Egyptian gate, and been drawn down the path to his obelisk as if by magnetism. But the real monument to Noah Webster is back up the Connecticut River Valley in Springfield, Massachusetts.

George and Charles Merriam, of West Brookfield, Massachusetts, bought the copyright to Webster's *Dictionary* after his death and had the tact and perspicacity to hire Webster's son-in-law Chauncey Goodrich, a professor at Yale, to oversee a revision. The dictionary was published in one volume in 1847. The Merriam-Webster building in Springfield is a substantial two-story red brick building with the initials NW intertwined in bas-relief, surrounded by laurel wreaths, over the door. On the first floor are the business and publicity offices, with relics in glass showcases (a copy of the *Compendious*; Charles Merriam's copy of Webster's original two-volume edition). The lexicography department is upstairs. It would be enough to make Noah Webster dance. In the center of the floor, covering an area the size of a small orchard, are the citation files—an alphabetical index of clippings showing the written words in all their contexts, stamped with the dates and the initials of lexicographers—and along the walls are shelves holding every edition of the unabridged (from 1864) and the collegiate (beginning in 1898), and above the files are source books: a multivolume Middle English dictionary, concordances to Christopher Marlowe, Herman Melville, Keats, Joyce. . . . Around the perimeter are the lexicographers' offices.

There are lexicographers specializing in various fields (geography, religion, law, music, trademarks), along with definers (definitions are vetted by several editors before going into the dictionary), daters, cross-referencers, pronouncers, and etymologists. (Early on, the Merriam brothers had brought in a German scholar to emend Webster's spurious etymologies.) One office holds the black books of E. Ward Gilman, with his notes for Web 3, and a shelf that overflows with usage manuals.

As Merriam-Webster points out on the copyright page of its dictionaries, any publisher can slap the name Webster onto its dictionary, but only Merriam-Webster, in the persons of George and Charles Merriam, dealt directly with Noah Webster's family; the others are like the variations on the Original Ray's Pizza, the mythical New York pizzeria, all trying to cash in on a famous name.

In Springfield, I got a tour of the office from Peter Sokolowski, who was hired by Merriam-Webster to edit a French-English dictionary and stayed on. He and his colleagues are the people behind (and on) the *Merriam-Webster* Web site. The unabridged dictionary is now online in an updated edition (Web 4? Web eternal?), which, like the original *Webster's*, is sold by subscription. (It's a lot cheaper than it was in Noah Webster's day. His two-volume magnum opus cost twenty dollars, which was a small fortune in 1828; a subscription to the online *Merriam-Webster* Unabridged is thirty dollars a year.) On the Web site, lexicographers pop up like gophers, inviting you to learn points of grammar and usage ("It is I" vs. "It's me," "Hopefully," "Flat adverbs"). There are word games, a word of the day, trending words (from the news), a blog. Some drudges! These people are having far too much fun to be lexicographers. The free online dictionary invites you to report where you found the word you're looking up. I was put off by that stuff at first—it's terrible to say, but when I am researching a word I am not looking for an interactive experience. I want it to be just me and my *Webster's*. But once I had penetrated to the heart of the valley of lexicography, to the editorial refrigerator in the lunchroom (a grouchy dater kicked us out), I melted.

"There *are* other dictionaries," Sokolowski allowed. I'd noticed a volume of *Funk & Wagnalls* on the shelf. He told me that after the great dictionary war of the sixties the *New York Times* and every other newspaper in the country and the AP dropped *Merriam-Webster's* and went with *Webster's New World*, issued by the World Publishing Company. Its offices were in Cleveland. I remember the globe bulging out the side of the building, a landmark just before the left turn onto West Boulevard. Besides the *Plain Dealer*, this was the only place in Cleveland where one might pursue a publishing career. I used to pass it on the way to the pool where I was a foot checker.

———

Spelling is the clothing of words, their outward visible sign, and even those who favor sweatpants in everyday life like to make a *bella figura*, as the Italians say—a good impression—in their prose. A misspelling undermines your authority. And an eye for the misspelled word can give you an edge in the workplace. It was a spelling mistake that gave me my first break at *The New Yorker*. Helen Stark had been right to predict that I would get restless in the editorial library. We took the magazine apart—figuratively, by summarizing its contents on index cards, and literally, with razor blades—and I wanted to help put

it together. There was an informal training program, and Helen
agreed to let me spend a few mornings a week on the nineteenth
floor, helping to read foundry proofs. Dave Jackson was the head
of foundry, and many proofreaders had started by working with
him. He was tall and thin with a hectic red complexion and
teeth that he could employ in a vicious grille. He looked like a
less fortunate Noël Coward. He worked in a narrow room near
the makeup department; earlier, his and his associate's desks had
been right in makeup. Foundry proofreading was the final reading before a piece went to print. Dave set me up at a desk with
an easel-like board and showed me how to compare the Reader's
proof, marked with changes from the day before, line for line
with the new version, to make sure that no mistakes had been
introduced by the printer. When there were no changes and the
copy didn't reflow, you just had to make sure no lines had been
dropped. You didn't even have to read the piece. In fact, no one
wanted your opinion. It was a strictly mechanical process: fold
the old proof lengthwise, line up the column of type with the
new proof, and move your pencil point down the page, eyeball-
ing only the first few letters of each line. I always tried to read
the whole line to try to catch a typo.

  "I see you also caught that misspelling of idiosyncrasy," Dave
said, approvingly, implying that only a fortunate few knew that
"idiosyncrasy" was spelled with an *s* at the end, not a *c*. Once he told
me that V. S. Pritchett was a "marvellous" (with two *New Yorker*
l's) writer but a terrible speller. Pritchett had spelled "skeptical"
with a *c* ("sceptical"), in the British fashion. Dave looked ferocious
when he pronounced on these matters. He taught me that "over
all" was two words as an adverb, as in "Over all, Dave gave me
a good education." Closed up, "overall" was an item of clothing

worn by a car mechanic. Also, it was "what ever," two words, as in "What *ever* happened to Baby Jane?" "Whatever" (one word) was a pronoun: "Whatever you do, don't introduce a mistake."

Dave's office was full of shopping bags that were full of books. Fire inspectors had visited his apartment and deemed it a firetrap, so every day he ferried a shopping bag full of books from his apartment, on the Upper West Side, to the office. One day, he offered me a paperback copy of *Wuthering Heights* that he had bought on the street. "I already have a copy, but I couldn't bear to leave it out there," he said, with his vicious grin.

I made my first big catch as a foundry proofreader in one of the Christmas shopping columns. The writer was in the basement of Bloomingdale's, shopping for food staples, and she had included in the list sacks of sugar and "flower." I circled the interior *we* and brought it out to the margin and suggested *u*, putting a question mark next to it, as I had been taught. The question mark was necessary not because there was any doubt that the writer meant "flour" instead of "flower" but because I was inserting something that had not been on the Reader's proof: that is, something that the OK'er, the proofreader of record, might have overlooked. If the typesetter made a mistake, you corrected it, no questions asked. But if a mistake had been carried over, the question mark on the foundry proof alerted the editor and the proofreader to something that might have slipped through. The question mark could be stricken and the change accepted, or both the question mark and the change crossed out and the change rejected. That question mark was a way of layering the sequence of changes, keeping a trail that showed the stage at which the change was made and whose idea it was. Without the question mark, a change could go straight

BETWEEN YOU & ME

to the printer without anyone in authority taking a second look. It was stupid to query something that betrayed your ignorance (and I did that, too), but it was occupational suicide to leave off the question mark and be responsible for a change that was not intended.

Checking my work, Dave Jackson drew his pencil through the entire word "flower" and brought the line out to the margin and wrote "flour," making my timid mark into something bolder, and then printed my initials firmly in the upper right-hand corner: MN.

I was thrilled to have found such a flagrant error, but dismayed to see my initials. Could there be a duller combination of letters of the alphabet? I had always printed my initials as MJN, which I thought was more elegant—my pen name was going to be M. J. Norris (though I hoped no one would figure out that my middle name was Jane). But I didn't have the nerve to correct Dave Jackson. He nipped out my middle initial, just like that, and baptized me into the culture of *The New Yorker.*

I went back down to the library, back to my paste pot and my single-edge razor blade and the special pen with white ink for printing writers' names in block letters on the spines of the black scrapbooks. I was proud of myself for finding that mistake, but I had to suppress any sign of excitement. Because no great intellectual effort was expected of me in the library, and the work so nearly resembled things I had done in kindergarten (albeit with blunt-edged scissors), I celebrated by going across the street to the Blue Bar at the Algonquin and having beer and peanuts for lunch. Later that week I got a note through interoffice mail. It said, "I thank you, the writer thanks you, Eleanor Gould thanks you, the proofreader thanks you, the fact checker thanks you, we all thank you for doing what we in all our numbers could not do: catching the flower for flour in the Christmas list on food." At the end were scrawled the initials GB: Gardner Botsford, the breezy, regal editor whom the men of the makeup department had told stories about on my very first day. It elated me. I had made my first catch.

Chapter 2
....

THAT WITCH!

I ALWAYS FORGET THAT, IN THE popular imagination, the copy editor is a bit of a witch, and it surprises me when someone is afraid of me. Not long ago, a young editorial assistant getting her first tour of the *New Yorker* offices paused at my door to be introduced, and when she heard I was a copy editor she jumped back, as if I might poke her with a red-hot hyphen or force-feed her a pound of commas. *Relax*, I wanted to say. I don't make a habit of correcting people in conversation or in print—unless it's for publication and they ask for it, or I'm getting paid.

We copy editors sometimes get a reputation for wanting to redirect the flow, change the course of the missile, have our way with a piece of prose. The image of the copy editor is of someone who favors a rigid consistency, a mean person who enjoys pointing out other people's errors, a lowly person who is just starting out on her career in publishing and is eager to make an impres-

sion, or, at worst, a bitter, thwarted person who wanted to be a
writer and instead got stuck dotting the *i*'s and crossing the *t*'s
and otherwise advancing the careers of other writers. I suppose
I have been all of these.

But good writers have a reason for doing things the way
they do them, and if you tinker with their work, taking it
upon yourself to neutralize a slightly eccentric usage or zap a
comma or sharpen the emphasis of something that the writer
was deliberately keeping obscure, you are not helping. In my
experience, the really great writers enjoy the editorial process.
They weigh queries, and they accept or reject them for good
reasons. They are not defensive. The whole point of having
things read before publication is to test their effect on a general
reader. You want to make sure when you go out there that the tag
on the back of your collar isn't poking up—unless, of course, you
are deliberately wearing your clothes inside out.

When the opening chapters of Philip Roth's *I Married a Communist* ran in *The New Yorker*, I got to OK it. It was immaculate,
partly because we were working from the galleys of the book:
copy editors at Farrar, Straus and Giroux had already been over
it, and, once a piece is in that form, authors, agents, and editors
are reluctant to change a ligature. I went over it, giving it all
I had: sometimes copy departments at publishing houses miss
something, just as we sometimes miss something. As it happens,
I noticed a small inconsistency in a passage that was quoted from
a children's history book. It was a long quotation, set off in small
type, and it was repeated at the end, with some slight variation.
I marked it and gave my proof to the fiction editor, Bill Buford.
Later, Bill's assistant came bounding up the stairs and delivered to me a color Xerox of the first page of my proof, on which

Buford had written in blue, "Of Mary Norris, Roth said: 'Who is this woman? And will she come live with me?'"

Up to that point, I'd read only *Goodbye, Columbus* and *Portnoy's Complaint*. Helen Stark had been all atwitter when *The Ghost Writer* ran in the magazine—she saved it for herself to index. Now I bought the audiobook of *I Married a Communist* and listened to it on a drive back from Ohio. It was read by the actor Ron Silver, and I almost went off the road during an ecstatic passage where the stars were furnaces: furnace of Ira, furnace of Eve. It seemed so warm and passionate. The book was funny, too: the hero is forced to schlep his girlfriend's daughter's harp all over town, and I had a harpist in the family, so I knew what a pain the harp was—there is nothing heavenly about a working harp. I subsequently had a year of Roth: *Patrimony, The Facts* ("Reader, I married her"), all the Zuckerman books. When *Exit Ghost* came out, I went back and read *The Ghost Writer.* I was on a trip to Amsterdam and saw Anne Frank's house and reread her diary while staying in a hotel on the spot of one that burned down during the war. I was so sorry when I ran out of Roth to read.

I did speak with Roth on the phone once, closing a piece about Saul Bellow, and saw him at a *New Yorker* Christmas party. I have been smitten ever since the proposition on the page proof. I suppose all he wanted was a housekeeper, someone to keep track of the details. But if he should ever read this I just want to say I'm still available.

———

There is a big fancy word for "going beyond your province": "ultracrepidate"—you'll find it in Web II. So much of copy editing is about not going beyond your province. Anti-ultra-crepidationism. Writers might think we're applying rules and sticking it to their prose in order to make it fit some standard, but just as often we're backing off, making exceptions, or at least trying to find a balance between doing too much and doing too little. A lot of the decisions you have to make as a copy editor are subjective. For instance, an issue that comes up all the time, whether to use "that" or "which," depends on what the writer means—it's interpretive, not mechanical.

Think of the great Dylan Thomas line "The force that through the green fuse drives the flower." It's a bit unfair to consider this as an example, because (1) it's poetry, and we can't all write (or drink) like Dylan Thomas, and (2) nobody remembers what comes next. It goes like this: "The force that through the green fuse drives the flower / Drives my green age." A gorgeous line. Although it is verse, and quoting any more of it would confuse the issue, it nevertheless passes the test for determining whether to use "that" or "which": if the phrase or clause introduced by a relative pronoun—"that" or "which"—is essential to the meaning of the sentence, "that" is preferred, and it is not separated from its antecedent by a comma. Maybe some inferior poet would write, "The force which through the green fuse drives the flower" (the audience at his reading would snort), or, worse, "The force, which through the green fuse drives the flower, / Drives my green age" (this writer would never make it into print, unless he hired a good copy editor). "The force" has no meaning without "that through the green fuse." Take it away and you are left with "The force . . . drives my green age," leaving you to wonder, What force? Which force? Are we watching *Star Wars*? "May the Force, which through the green fuse drives the flower, be with you." I can hear Bill Murray saying this, but not Dylan Thomas or Luke Skywalker.

I am bending over backwards not to use the term "restrictive," because the associations with the word "restrictive" are so discouraging. Clothing is restrictive. Dietary restrictions may apply. Restrictive regulations would prevent you from, say, fishing off a runway at Kennedy Airport or swimming in the ocean when the lifeguards are not on duty. "To restrict" (*Webster's*) is "to confine within bounds." I don't know about you, but I chafe at restrictions.

Even the dictionary citation illustrating a "restrictive clause" is a bummer: *Webster's* gives the example of "that you ordered" in the sentence "The book that you ordered is out of print." Oh, no! The *Random House College Dictionary* has a slightly more positive definition for the grammatical sense of restrictive—"of or pertaining to a word, phrase, or clause that identifies or limits the meaning of a modified element"—but it goes on to give yet another bummer of an example: "*that just ended* in *The year that just ended was bad for crops.*" Just my luck: the book that I wanted is out of print, and now the price of corn is going to skyrocket.

I don't mean to make this any more confusing than it already is, but let's not pretend it's easy. Here is the *Random House College Dictionary* on nonrestrictive: "pertaining to a word, phrase, or clause that describes or supplements a modified element but is not essential in establishing its identity, as the relative clause *which has been dry* in the sentence *This year, which has been dry, was bad for crops.* In English, a nonrestrictive clause is usu. set off by commas." This is admirably clear, but we're still suffering from a drought.

Do you see the difference between "The year that just ended

was bad for crops" and "This year, which has been dry, was bad for crops"? With "this year," we already know which year the writer is talking about: you could write with perfect clarity, "This year was bad for crops." You could also write, "The year was bad for crops," but in the context you'd need to know what year was meant; adding "that just ended" identifies the year.

"Nonrestrictive" has a nicer ring to it than "restrictive." I like nonrestrictive clothing and a nonrestrictive diet. Here is the definition from Web II of a nonrestrictive clause: "An adjective clause which adds information but is so loosely attached to its noun as to be not essential to the definiteness of the noun's meaning (the aldermen, *who were present*, assented)—called also *descriptive clause*. Such a clause is marked off by commas, whereas the corresponding restrictive clause is not (the aldermen *who were present* assented = such aldermen as were present assented)." Of course, the hilarious thing about this is that the definition itself uses "which" ("an adjective clause *which* adds information") where standard modern American usage prefers "that": "an adjective clause *that* adds information."

I always have to pause and think what I mean by restrictive: you think something that is restrictive is going to take the commas, that the commas will restrict the clause, cordon it off, keep it out of the way. But it is just the opposite: a restrictive clause is so much a part of the noun it modifies that it doesn't need any punctuation to stake its claim. The original purpose of a comma was to separate, and a restrictive clause does not want to be separate from what it modifies: it wants to be one with it, to be essential to it, to identify with it totally. Once you get the idea of what is restrictive (She was a graduate of a school that had very high standards), everything else is nonrestrictive (He graduated from another school, which would admit anyone with a pulse).

If people are nervous, they sometimes use "which" when "that" would do. Politicians often say "which" instead of "that," to sound important. A writer may say "which" instead of "that"— it's no big deal. It would be much worse to say "that" instead of "which." Apparently the British use "which" more and do not see anything wrong with it. Americans have agreed to use "that" when the clause is restrictive and to use "which," set off with commas, when the clause is nonrestrictive. It works pretty well.

An excellent example of a clause that everyone knows and that could be either restrictive or nonrestrictive is in the Lord's Prayer: Our Father, who art in Heaven (Matthew 6:9). Is "who art in Heaven" restrictive or nonrestrictive? Just where is God? I think it is nonrestrictive, as indicated by the comma before "who"; that is, the phrase "who art in Heaven" doesn't define the Father, it just tells where he lives. It is as if you could insert "by the way": "Our Father, who, by the way, resides in Heaven"— except that "Our Father" is vocative, the grammatical term for direct address. In direct address there is no need to tell God where he is. In the original context, Jesus taught this prayer to his disciples. If there are no commas, the implication is that whoever is praying has another father (Joseph?). So conceivably Christ intended the phrase "who art in Heaven" as restrictive, to identify the heavenly father as opposed to the earthly one. Putting theology aside for a moment, I might say, speaking for my siblings and me, "our father, who art in Cleveland." We would all understand that I was talking about our one and only dad, in Cleveland. New Testament Greek did without the commas, and the sense of it, in translation, has been up for grabs ever since.

The Latin, which comes to us from Saint Jerome, is *"Pater noster, qui es in caelis."* Nonrestrictive. You can *hear* the commas. The English translation, from the Book of Common Prayer (1662), makes it "Our Father, which art in Heaven." Nonrestrictive, and thanks for the "which," Anglicans, even if you did later change it to "who." God here is the Creator, the Father in a figurative sense, and in a monotheistic tradition there is only one. But a modern Anglican version, dating from 1988, makes it simply "Our Father in heaven," which is restrictive: our heavenly father, not our earthly one. One modern English version, both Catholic and Anglican, from 1928, does without the comma: "Our Father who art in heaven." It's a little weird, you have to admit: the restrictive one, without the commas, is more direct; it almost goes out of its way to snub the earthly father. The nonrestrictive, with the commas, is acknowledging that he is the father of us all and making note of his whereabouts.

I'm not religious. But isn't this nearly mystical?

———

After my first big catch at *The New Yorker*, I latched onto the coattails of my friend Nancy Holyoke, whom I'd met in the editorial library, where we'd both been initiated into the sisterhood of the rubber thumb. She had moved up to collating, and finally, after three years of indexing, I got a chance to join her in that department. In collating you transferred changes from the editor, the writer, the proofreaders (usually two), and the fact checker onto a clean proof for the printer. It was not a job I was born for: it demanded legible handwriting, and my penmanship had been deteriorating since third grade.

The good thing about collating was that you learned how the place ran: collating was the nexus, it was where everything came together. From copying the changes of proofreaders, I learned what proofreaders did. I got into trouble for abridging the tedious queries of the libel lawyer (they should have made a rubber stamp). I learned *New Yorker* style on things like numbers by having to write out "three hundred and sixty-five dollars a week." "But that's wrong," I said to Nancy when she was training me. I knew from writing checks that the proper formulation was "three hundred sixty-five dollars," without the "and." Nancy's reply was "Nevertheless, that is the way it's done." It sounded kind of haughty, but she made it clear to me that unless I got with the program I was going nowhere. When Nancy asked, "Do you want me to tell you your mistakes?" I said yes, and was chagrined to learn that I had misread a checker's proof and put a hyphen into a word that was meant to be closed up. In collating, I learned to check my work three times, a page at a time: line by line, as I was doing it; then again, line by line, after I'd finished the page; and finally, mechanically, one more time, by looking not at the text but at the changes, starting at the top of the page and moving clockwise down one margin, across the bottom, and up the other. You had to be willing to admit that you were capable of missing something or you would not catch what you'd missed.

Ed Stringham, the head of the collating department, had been at *The New Yorker* for decades and had grown a hump on his back in the service of the magazine. He came into the office most days at about 3 p.m. He had an ambitious reading agenda, which he charted in a series of black-and-white composition books. He supplemented his reading with the art and the music of whatever culture he was into at the time. He had started with

Greece, moved on to Rome, and approached every country in Europe methodically: France, Germany, Spain, Iceland, Norway, Sweden, Denmark, the Faeroe Islands. He became especially involved in the literature of countries behind the Iron Curtain: Poland, Czechoslovakia, Hungary, Romania. He was jaded about *The New Yorker*. When something came out in the magazine that he really wanted to read (a translation of *Man in the Holocene*, by the Swiss writer Max Frisch, for example), he waited for it to appear in book form, because he couldn't enjoy anything that was printed in *The New Yorker*'s twelve-point Caslon type. He divided up any work that came into the office, even if it was just two pages; for longer pieces he used long division. When the work was done, he stayed at the office, reading at his big slanted desk—more like a drafting table—or in his tattered armchair, smoking cigarettes and spilling sugar packets into and around a cup of takeout coffee. His assistant, me (they made a little show of calling me his "associate"), sat at a desk in a small annex. Ed may have been the model for the character called the Ghost in Jay McInerney's book *Bright Lights, Big City*: a pale, white-haired man who roams the halls at night. I recognized him in Jack Kerouac's *The Dharma Bums*. He had known Kerouac and Ginsberg at Columbia, and after a drink or two he would start saying things like "Dig it, man."

The big challenge in collating was what were called Gould proofs. Eleanor Gould was a legendary *New Yorker* grammarian and query proofreader. She was a certified genius—a member not just of Mensa but of some über-group within Mensa—and Mr. Shawn had complete faith in her. She read everything in galley—everything except fiction, that is, which she had been taken off of years earlier, as I understood it, because she treated everyone the same, be it Marcel Proust or Annie Proulx, Nabokov or Malcolm Gladwell. Clarity was Eleanor's lodestar, *Fowler's Modern English* her bible, and by the time she was done with a proof the pencil lines on it looked like dreadlocks. Some of the fact pieces were ninety columns long, and Mr. Shawn took every query. My all-time favorite Eleanor Gould query was on Christmas gifts for children: the writer had repeated the old saw that every Raggedy Ann doll has "I love you" written on her little wooden heart, and Eleanor wrote in the margin that it did not, and she knew, because as a child she had performed open-heart surgery on her rag doll and seen with her own eyes that nothing was written on the heart.

Lu Burke sat in the office next to Eleanor's, her desk facing a wall that James Thurber had drawn on in pencil—a self-portrait, a football player, a man slumped over a typewriter. She was a proofreader and proud of it. "Not everyone can read proof," she used to say. Lu had worked at *Life*. At *The New Yorker* she read the fiction, valuing the writer's voice over correct usage, and edited the cartoon captions and the newsbreaks, those column fillers that *The New Yorker* ran, making fun of other publications' mistakes and making us acutely self-conscious about our own mistakes. "Are the glory years of *The New Yorker* gone forever?" This was the single typewritten line of a letter from a reader, seared in memory, sent in with a clipping from our pages, in which "chaise longue" had been erroneously rendered "chaise lounge." (That's how we said it in Ohio.) In her crisp, inimitable hand, Lu had added her own comment—"They certainly are!"—and circulated the letter. I never made that mistake again.

Lu wore Earth shoes and bluejeans and long-sleeved pullovers and stud earrings. She had short gray hair and snappy blue eyes. She patrolled the halls like a prison warden—you could almost see the ring of keys at her side—and she terrorized anyone new in the copy department. She had a jeweler's eye for print, and kept a loupe on her desk. Also on her desk was a canister, with a perforated lid, about the size of a shaker for red-pepper flakes in a pizzeria, wrapped in brown paper, on which she had drawn commas and the words "Comma Shaker." This was Lu's comment on *The New Yorker*'s "close" style of punctuation: she thought we used too many commas. Instead of *Fowler's*, she preferred a slim volume called *Mind the Stop*. Lu thought that elements of *New Yorker* style were ridiculous; for instance, our habit of putting points in I.B.M. when IBM itself had long since done without them, and of sticking a comma in Time, Inc., as if oblivious of the publisher's own practice (and of the pun on "ink"). Yet there was no more zealous enforcer.

In almost every way Lu was the opposite of Eleanor. She would never make what she called "a wooden fix." Eleanor might bend a sentence to her own logic; Lu would give it its head. Another colleague, Alice Quinn, once told me how Lu had explained the editorial process: "First we get the rocks out, Alice. Then we get the pebbles out. Then we get the sand out, and the writer's voice rises. No harm done." I could picture Lu peering at Alice with her snappy blue eyes, as if she were amusing herself by trying to scare a child. Her proofs, like her manner and her handwriting, were crisp and persuasive (all right, she was a bully). If you laid something in front of her on the desk to ask a question—maybe something subtle about an antecedent—her eye would light on an egregious error, and she'd say, "Get rid of that *o*," pointing to a hideous misspelling of "memento."

The only time you had to use your judgment in collating

was when there was a conflict between, say, the author and a proofreader, and the editor hadn't been clear about which change he preferred, or when the author or a checker added something: it hadn't gone through the copydesk, so it had to be styled. One of the first decisions I had to make was how to style "copy edit." I made it one word: "copyedit." The next day, Eleanor Gould not only undid my change in a revise of the piece but issued a style memo: henceforth "copy editor" was two words as a noun, hyphenated as a verb—"to copy-edit." It was uncanny: every time I had to make a decision and went with my instinct, I did the opposite of what Eleanor Gould would have done.

The great minefield in collating was a proof from the author, because that is where collating overlapped into copy editing (two words as a gerund). My job was to slavishly (and legibly) copy what was on the proof—I was a scribe—and not to correct or corrupt the text. But surely I wasn't meant to copy errors. And nobody would appreciate it if I did something obtrusive like insert a question mark in brackets. Everyone would wonder where it came from. It was one thing to correct a spelling—make sure there were two *n*'s in "annihilate," for instance—and another to judge what the author meant if he wrote that something or other was "immanent." Was that a mistake? Or a philosophical position? I've never met a usage of "immanent" that made the word's meaning clear to me. I took one such question to Eleanor Gould, who read it and said, in her slightly braying but kindly voice, "It sounds pretty imminent to me."

Often a word would come up that I had never seen before and could not find in the dictionary. That didn't mean it wasn't there—I just couldn't see it, probably because I didn't want to see it. I had a skeptical streak and an ego, and at some level I thought that if *I* had never seen a particular word it didn't exist. One year in the Christmas list on food, the writer inserted the word "terrine," as in "a terrine of foie gras." I had never seen the word "terrine" (much less an actual terrine full of foie gras) and couldn't find it in the dictionary, neither the Little Red Web nor the unabridged. So I changed it to "tureen." I might as well have changed it to "punchbowl." It was no excuse that I came from a family that didn't eat a lot of pâté. (The fanciest thing we had on the table was Brown 'n Serve rolls, which we called Black 'n Serve rolls, because my mother usually burned them. A college friend made merciless fun of me in the dining hall when I complained that the butter tasted funny and it came out that I had been raised on margarine.) Fortunately, the structure of the department was such that several people, including the author, read the proofs the next day, and the word appeared in the magazine as "terrine."

———

When I finally made it to the copydesk, it was a long time before I could once again read for pleasure. I spontaneously copy-edited everything I laid eyes on. I had a paperback edition of Faulkner's *The Hamlet* that was so riddled with typos that it almost ruined Flem Snopes for me. But, as I relaxed on the copydesk, I was sometimes even able to enjoy myself. There were writers who weren't very good and yet were impossible to improve, like figure skaters who hit all the technical marks but have a limited artistic appeal and sport unflattering costumes. There were competent writers on interesting subjects who were just careless enough in their spelling and punctuation to keep a girl occupied. And there were writers whose prose came in so highly polished that I couldn't believe I was getting paid to read them: John Updike, Pauline Kael, Mark Singer, Ian Frazier! In a way, these were the hardest, because the prose lulled me into complacency. They transcended the office of the copy editor. It was hard to stay alert for opportunities to meddle in an immaculate manuscript, yet if you missed something you couldn't use that as an excuse. The only thing to do was style the spelling, and even that could be fraught. Oliver Sacks turned out to be attached to the spelling of "sulphur" and "sulphuric" that he remembered from his chemistry experiments as a boy. (*The New Yorker* spelled it less romantically: "sulfur," "sulfuric.") Early on, I worked on a piece by Nora Ephron, a parody of frequent-flier rules titled "Dear Frequent Travelers." *The New Yorker* doubles the *l* in "travellers," and I doubted that an airline would—it looked more corporate without the extra letter. So I left it alone. Lu Burke came along behind me and doubled the *l*, probably while grumbling something about incompetent copy editors. I got no credit for being overscrupulous.

When Pauline Kael typed "prevert" instead of "pervert," she meant "prevert" (unless she was reviewing something by Jacques Prévert). Luckily, she was kind, and if you changed it she would just change it back and stet it without upbraiding you. Kael revised up until closing, and though we lackeys resented writers who kept changing "doughnut" to "coffeecake" then back to "doughnut" and then "coffeecake" again, because it meant more work for us, Kael's changes were always improvements. She approached me once in the makeup department with a proof in her hand. She couldn't figure out how to fix something, and I was the only one around. She knew me from chatting in the ladies' room on the eighteenth floor. I looked at the proof and made a suggestion, and she was delighted. "You *helped* me!" she gasped.

I was on the copydesk when John McPhee's pieces on geology were set up. I got to copy-edit "In Suspect Terrain," which is about I-80, my I-80, a road I know well: it is the road between Ohio and the George Washington Bridge, between my parents' house and my independence. I-80 took a long time to build. When I first came east to college, in New Jersey, in 1970, my father and I took the Pennsylvania Turnpike. We couldn't resist the exit for Norristown, and stayed in the King of Prussia Motel and ate at a Horn & Hardart. (I loved automats, with their selection of sandwiches and slices of pie behind miniature windows that you could open yourself.) The next year, I-80 was open as far as the Delaware Water Gap. We stopped there to eat the sandwiches my mother had packed, and though I have stopped there many times since, I have never found the spot my father and I happened on that first time, with its majestic beauty by the side of the road. Either that or it never looked as spectacular to me again. Every year, I-80 stretched farther east, until I no longer had to wind down Route 46 along the Delaware River. Now, of course, I like to get off I-80 and find new routes through New Jersey.

Copy-editing McPhee, I tried to keep my head. There was not much to do. McPhee was like John Updike, in that he turned in immaculate copy, and his editor, Pat Crow, he of the green rubber boots in the elevator, was neat and decisive. Really, all I had to do was read. I'd heard that McPhee compared his manuscript with the galleys, so anything *The New Yorker* did he noticed. I just looked up words in the dictionary to check the spelling (which was invariably correct, but I had to check) and determined whether compound words were hyphenated, whether hyphenated words should be closed up or printed as two words, or whether I should stet the hyphen. It was my province to capitalize the *I* in Interstate 80, hyphenate I-80, and lowercase "the interstate."

But in Part II of "In Suspect Terrain" I came to this sentence and thought I might have spotted an error: "But rock columns are generalized; they are atremble with hiatuses; and they depend in large part on well borings, which are shallow, and on seismic studies, which are new, and far between." The itchy-fingered copy editor hovered at the threshold. I wanted to let her in. I wasn't going to touch the comma, but I was desperate to correct that "new, and far between" to "few, and far between." I could save McPhee from making a horrible mistake! But many people with finer minds than mine were lined up to read the copy when I was through, beginning with Eleanor Gould and finishing with a phalanx of proofreaders. They would not assume that "new" was a typo for "few," and if they had any doubt they could query it, asking the author through his editor, and there would be no harm done. But I was hellbent on rectifying what might be a glitch in a cliché. It was a Friday—I remember, because I knew that if I made this change I would have to live all weekend with the possibility, which could swiftly morph into a certainty, that I had made a mistake. Two mistakes: I would have gone beyond my province, and I would have introduced an error into McPhee's carefully wrought prose.

So I stayed my hand, the itchy-fingered hand with the pencil in it, and spent the weekend with a clean conscience. As soon as I left the office, I felt relieved that I had let it alone. What ever made me think that McPhee would misspell, or even mistype, the word "few"?

Another common problem that demands judgement is the dangling participle. With a dangler, you can either fix the subject of the sentence to match the participle or give the participial phrase its own verb, turning it into a clause.

My favorite example of a dangler is the road sign for weigh stations: "Trucks Enter When Flashing." A participial phrase generally attaches to the subject: so although we know that "Trucks Enter When Flashing" means that when the light is flashing the trucks must enter, grammatically it's the trucks that are flashing. Fishing around for an example of a properly used participle, I think of a minnow wriggling on a hook and what it might say as the game fish approaches: "Looking up, I noticed I was bait." See? The participial phrase, "Looking up," attaches to the subject, "I."

A lot of people are not bothered by danglers, and even good writers occasionally slip up. A good writer who is also stubborn might cling to a dangler, pretend she did it on purpose, because she knows what she means and she thinks the sentence communicates that. This writer is clinging to a rope that has failed to swing her to the next branch. For many danglers, there is no obvious perfect fix, which can make the writer, and sometimes the editor, want to retain the original, even if it's technically flawed.

Once I objected to the sentence "Over tea in the greenhouse, her mood turned dark." The editor said, testily, "Can't we just leave it?" I insisted that her mood wasn't hovering over the tea (well, maybe it was, but I was feeling literal-minded that day). The sentence became "As we drank tea in the greenhouse, her mood turned dark." It's not anything that jumps out, but there is something more brooding about the version with the dangler.

The better the writer, the more complicated the dangler. Here is a sentence from the novelist Edward St. Aubyn, an excellent writer: "Walking down the long, easily washed corridors of his grandmother's nursing home, the squeak of the nurse's rubber soles made his family's silence seem more hysterical than it was." It seems shrewish to find fault with one sentence out of the millions of exquisitely wrought ones in a 680-page compilation of four novels by a prose wizard. But I'm going to anyway. It was not the "squeak" that was "walking down the long, easily washed corridors" (and yes, that phrase conjures up the underpaid mopper of corridors and the layer of hard wax, like corn, over the faint, ineradicable scent of urine), or even "the nurse's rubber soles" (so hideously clinical), but the "nurse," who is buried in a possessive.

The editor who would dare tinker with this sentence has two options: she can try an active verb in the participial phrase ("As the nurse walked down the long, easily washed corridors of his grandmother's nursing home, the squeak of her rubber soles . . ."). Or she can try to change the main clause so that the subject is the thing modified by the participial phrase: "Walking down the long, easily washed corridors of his grandmother's nursing home, the nurse in her squeaky rubber soles . . ." Well, good luck with that. It's the squeak, not the nurse, that makes the silence seem hysterical. Nothing I can do would improve this sentence. If it had been pointed out to the author, he might have rewritten it or he might have said he didn't see anything wrong with it. So it turns out there is a third option: do nothing. Sometimes it's easier to reconcile oneself to the dangler than it is to fix it. In this instance, maybe the queasiness created by the dangler, that sense of imbalance, whether or not one knows the reason for it, helps convey the sensation of walking down the corridor of the dreaded nursing home.

Not too long ago, in a piece by the incomparable George Saunders, I had to deal with a dangler. Saunders writes fiction, and often his narrative voice is not an educated one. After spending two days on a piece written in the form of the diary of a well-meaning but benighted family man ("The Semplica-Girl Diaries"), I found myself thinking in Saunders's fragments. Guy sounds like some kind of hick. Inner dialogue like Tarzan. Go home, take strong drink, preferably Negroni (gin, not vodka). Next day, try again.

The story had in its first column a dangler that, even knowing that people use danglers, I found it hard not to want to fix: "While picking kids up at school, bumper fell off Park Avenue." Technically, in Saunders's sentence, the bumper is picking the kids up at school. ("Park Avenue" refers to an old Buick.) The fix, though, would do violence to the voice—the narrator's diary is written in note-taking fashion, so the subject is often left out ("Stood looking up at house, sad"). The easiest fix for the bumper sentence is to put a subject into the introductory phrase, making a proper clause out of it—"While I was picking the kids up at school"—but this would drain the sentence of character. You may wish that Tarzan had gone to school, or at least been exposed to educational TV, but you wouldn't want to change his diction. As the piece is written in a telegraphic style, I could tell myself that the "I was" was implied, and therefore the bumper was being propped up invisibly (until it fell off).

The piece also had numbers in it—that is, numerals—which I instinctively didn't touch. No styling $200 into two hundred dollars when a guy is doing his household budget in his diary. He also uses plus signs and equal signs. He does not put quotation marks around speech. His object is to set down "a picture of life and times" for "future people." He does not need to prettify it. Let him say "hopefully" instead of "it is to be hoped that," leave the parentheses within parentheses [brackets would be worse], don't expect him to put commas around "too," in "he too once had car whose bumper fell off."

One thing I cannot let go of is the spelling. There were a few deliberate misspellings ("herts," "dauhter"), attributed to a child, that I knew to stet, but there were also spellings that were not wrong, just different, and that the author might not want to change. For instance, we prefer the fancy spelling of "catalogue," ending in *ue*, and, as I said, we double the unstressed consonant before a suffix: "totalling," "traveller." (My autocorrect only very reluctantly tolerates these extra *l*'s.) Fortunately, George Saunders is not on autocorrect, and he accepted these curlicues. The narrator wouldn't use them, but the reader doesn't notice. In fact, a *New Yorker* reader might notice if we left them out, and the point is not to let the orthography distract the reader from the meaning.

I stopped short of querying the spelling of the name of the narrator's daughter Lilly. I would have spelled it with just one *l*, but she's not my daughter; she's the daughter of a narrator voiced by George Saunders, and who knows better than that narrator what he wrote on his daughter's birth certificate? Yet when a character says that his company will "garner" the narrator's wages and is corrected by the narrator's wife, Pam—"Garnish," she says, harshly—I can't resist taking it to the next level. "To garnish" is to finish off a cocktail by adding, say, a slice of orange (where is that Negroni?); the correct term here is "garnishee." True, under "garnish" *Webster's* lists "garnishee," but it is our style to use the spelling preferred by *Webster's*—the word printed in boldface and accorded a full definition—not the word in small caps buried under another word. *Webster's* includes a lot of words that people spell and use in nonstandard ways. (Lu Burke once jumped all over me because she thought that I had let "minuscule" go spelled with two *i*'s because *Webster's* includes the barbarous spelling "miniscule" to guide people to the right one.) So I garnish my proof with this query. My reasoning is that Pam is correcting someone, and she is smarter than her husband, so shouldn't she get it right?

The editor dutifully passed the query along to the author, and later told me that he turned it down, saying, "I don't think this guy should know more than I do."

Fair enough. Garnishee my wages. Anyway, spelling not point. Point is words—right words in right order, for devastating effect. Job of copy editor is to spell words right: put hyphen in, take hyphen out. Repeat. Respect other meaning of spell: spell writer weaves.

Chapter 3
....

THE PROBLEM OF HEESH

I HAVE ALWAYS CONFUSED SEX AND gender. From the
moment that Sister Mary Abram instructed us in French
class that the table (*la table*) was feminine, I have been dubious.
I wanted to know why, and she couldn't give me a reason. She
tried to get it through my head that language isn't logical—or,
rather, that certain idioms are not reducible to logic. There's no
reason that the table is feminine: it just is—always was, ever shall
be. So many things in language can never be known or settled
or explained, except by custom. This same Sister Abram once
defied anyone to tell her she couldn't say "my most favoritist
thing." The gender of *la table* might not change, but the meaning
of gender would, as would Sister Mary Abram, shedding the Old
Testament name and jettisoning the habit, and busting out of the
convent to become a hot chick whose most favoritist thing was
smoking cigarettes.

In my junior year of college, I took a course called Women in Literature, with Elaine Showalter, a trailblazer in the field of women's studies. It was a contentious time. The honorific "Ms." had just been coined, Gloria Steinem had recently started *Ms.* magazine, and Norman Mailer was brawling with feminists at Town Hall. But feminism was new to me, and I had it confused with wearing pants and hating my mother and being bitter toward men. In class, we read the seminal works by women: *The Yellow Wallpaper, A Room of One's Own, Slouching Towards Bethlehem.* (Back then, someone would have taken exception to the word "seminal" in that context; what did semen have to do with it?) And one of the things we discussed was sexist language. Was it an insult to be called a "woman writer"? Didn't it have a taint of, say, the "woman driver"?

In an era when a woman could be anything—a chef, an astronaut, a Supreme Court justice—the traditional feminine forms of vocation words ("hostess," "waitress," "usherette") were becoming obsolete. H. W. Fowler, compiling his *Dictionary of Modern English Usage* at the dawn of women's suffrage (he would have preferred the term "female suffrage"), held the well-intentioned view that as more women found their way into the workplace, taking traditionally masculine jobs, the need for "feminine designations" would grow. But it didn't work out that way. "Authoress" had never been popular—from Victorian times, it sounded patronizing. And no female poet I know has ever wanted to be called a "poetess" (or, for that matter, a "female poet"). In English, the feminine suffix has a whiff of the diminutive, as if to say, "The little lady sometimes turns her hand to poesy."

By now, "Ms." is surprisingly well established (even *Ms.* magazine is still around), and "actress" and "comedienne" have been largely subsumed by the uninflected "actor" and "comedian."

In some cases, we've switched over to a new, gender-neutral job description. When men started slinging coffee on airplanes, "stewardess" gave way to "flight attendant"; in restaurants, we now have "servers"; the mail is delivered by "postal carriers." David Marsh, an Irishman who is the usage expert for the *Guardian*, proposes that where a person's sex makes a difference "the words male and female are perfectly adequate," and offers as an example the Grammy category "best international female artist." But there is no agreement even on which adjective to use, and some women bristle, in certain contexts, at being called female: it seems to focus exclusively on the reproductive system, and makes you feel like a chicken, all thighs and breasts.

I've heard people refer to a "lady doctor" and a "lady dentist," an odd overlay of the aristocratic and the biological on the vocational. On the male side, there is "gentleman farmer," which means rich and landed. ("Lady farmer" doesn't have the same effect, but "lady rancher" would work.) "Male nurse," "male stripper," and "male prostitute" are all crossover terms, indicating that men are making inroads into female strongholds. Generally, in English, to have your sex tacked onto your occupation is unnecessary and often insulting. Except for the handful of professions defined by biology, like wet nurse and midwife and madam, why should sex enter into it? There are a few imperishable English words where the feminine ending is strong and useful—"heroine," from the Greek, and, from the Latin, "dominatrix." Take that, sexist pigs.

———

Sister Abram could have saved us both a lot of grief if she had quoted what Robert Graves and Alan Hodge wrote on the sub-

ject of gender in *The Reader Over Your Shoulder*: "English . . .
has certain unusual advantages in structure. In the first place,
it is almost uninflected and has no genders. The Romance
and Germanic languages, not having had occasion to simplify
themselves to the same degree, still retain their genders and
inflections. They are a decorative survival from a primitive time
when the supposed sex of all concepts—trees, diseases, cooking
implements—had to be considered for the sake of religious convention or taboo."

A little farther in, Graves adds something that, had I heard
it from Sister Abram in 1969, might have made the course of my
education less fraught: "Gender is illogical, in being used partly
to express actual sex, e.g. *le garçon, la femme,* and partly to dress
words up, e.g. *la masculinité, le féminisme; le festin, la fête.*" Note
that "masculinity" is feminine and "feminism" is masculine.

I have never had a gift for divining the gender of a noun
in a foreign language. I almost invariably get it wrong. Not
long ago, I came upon a notebook that I kept in an effort to
master the genders of nouns in Modern Greek. They come in
masculine, feminine, and neuter, as in Latin and German, and
they have endings that sometimes offer a clue (-omicron sigma
for masculine, -eta for feminine, -omicron for neuter), but just
as often are deceptive. Many of the words have decayed since
antiquity—a sigma has fallen off—so a word might look neuter
yet retain its ancient gender, which might, despite a masculine-
looking ending, have been feminine all along. Determined to get
this gender thing under control, I marked each noun with the
symbols from alchemy: a circle with arrow pointing up, as if with
an erection, for masculine; a circle with cross descending, as if
in childbirth, for feminine. I had to invent a symbol for neuter:

a circle with both the arrow and the cross, and a slash through it, as on a "no pedestrians" sign. It was pathetic. It looked as if I were trying to lock the nouns up in cages.

Later, when I studied Italian, I used free association as a mnemonic device, laboriously memorizing the gender of every word, one at a time. It was easy enough with the equivalents of our vocation words. In Italian, *poetessa* is not an insult; it is simply the feminine form of "poet," as *dottoressa, contessa, professoressa* are feminine forms of "doctor," "count," "professor." But the word *bicchiere*, say, meaning "glass": how could I remember that it was masculine? Sounds like beaker, which reminds me of chemistry and of Louis Pasteur, a chemist, who was a man: ergo *bicchiere* was masculine. But sometimes the beaker would remind me of Madame Curie, also a chemist, who was a woman, and I'd get confused. For *bottiglia*, "bottle," if the *a* at the end wasn't enough to tell me it was feminine, I could think of a bottle of beer with the St. Pauli girl on it. *Latte*, "milk," was masculine, which seemed counterintuitive, because it's the woman who lactates. I fell back on my experience as a milkman: *latte*, masculine. Obviously, if you grow up in a gendered language, you digest these forms along with your mother's (masculine) milk, and perhaps if I had been given Latin to play with as a child I'd have had an easier time with the concept of gender later in life.

English carries a secret burden of gender. We traditionally refer to a ship as "she"—perhaps not so much now, in the abstract, but as soon as we grow fond of a particular boat "it" becomes "she," and probably has a feminine name. I might refer to my car in the feminine: She is getting old, the Éclair. When I was studying the harp, my teacher, whose living room was full of concert harps—gilded, ebony, bird's-eye maple—told me that harps, like ships, are "she"s. Can it be a coincidence that these are all feminine nouns in Italian? *La nave, la macchina, l'arpa.* We speak of the mother tongue (the Latin *lingua* and the Greek *glossa* are both feminine) and the mother country (but also of the fatherland). The United States is said to be a daughter of Great Britain. The feminine is just below the surface, and so is the masculine. In 1993, when Lorena Bobbitt cut off the penis of her husband, the aptly named John Wayne Bobbitt, a famous writer who shall go nameless was assigned to cover her trial for *The New Yorker.* His piece (which never ran) circulated around the office in samizdat. In the passage that described what Lorena Bobbitt did, on leaving the house, when she realized that she still had her husband's penis clutched in her hand, the author wrote that "she threw him into a field." Well, of course the penis is a male appendage, but to spontaneously assign it grammatical gender seems to me proof of two things: a man's attachment to his penis, and the fact that that attachment runs right down to his linguistic roots. They don't call them personal pronouns for nothing.

Pronouns run deep. A friend's father once said to her, "Don't call your mother 'she.'" My friend wondered why not—it was accurate—but to her father it sounded disrespectful: his daughter was dismissing her mother with a mere pronoun, "a poor little weak thing of only three letters," as Mark Twain wrote of the German pronoun *sie* in his essay "The Awful German Language." Or perhaps my friend's father thought she was subtly suggesting that father and daughter were allied against the mother in a conspiracy of pronouns. But why would "she" be an insult? How can a pronoun resound in so many ways? In German, every noun as well as every article (both definite and indefinite) and adjective may change form depending on its gender as well as on its case, and there are three genders (masculine, feminine, and neuter) and four cases (nominative, accusative, dative, and genitive). So that's a lot to master. (Twain had the same problem I do with gender. In the same essay, he wrote, "Every noun has a gender, and there is no sense or system in the distribution; so the gender of each must be learned separately and by heart. There is no other way. To do this one has to have a memory like a memorandum-book. In German, a young lady has no sex, while a turnip has. Think what overwrought reverence that shows for the turnip, and what callous disrespect for the girl.")

There are subtle distinctions in pronouns from language to language. We no longer use the familiar form of "you"—"thou," "thee," "thine"—while German and Italian, for example, carry on distinguishing the familiar forms (*du* and *tu*) from the formal *Sie* and *Lei*. The formal "you" is capitalized in German and Italian, while the first-person singular (*ich* and *io*) is lowercase: what does that say about how people think of themselves in relation to others in German and Italian as opposed to the way they do in English, where the convention is reversed? Actually, Italians don't even use the pronouns if they don't feel like it, because the verb forms have that information packed into them. Japanese does without gender entirely. Highly inflected verb forms signal the relationships between the speaker (bossy if a man, meek if a woman) and the spoken to and the spoken of. Sometimes, a Japanese person with good English still confuses "he," "she," and "it," to our delight. In a 2010 documentary about John Lennon, Yoko Ono remembered giving a beautiful silk pajama (she used the singular) to John. "She fit him totally," Yoko said.

Our language problems with gender are not as complicated as German or as exotic as John Lennon's silk pajama, but they are endlessly controversial. Perhaps the most intractable problem hovers around the conventional use of the masculine pronoun to include the feminine when the antecedent is mixed (he or she) or unknown or irrelevant. As the last bastion of grammatical gender in the English language, the third-person-singular personal pronouns—"he," "she," "him," "her," "his," "hers"—these six dense and ancient words, rounded with wear into tough little nuts, have become the most ticklish subject in modern English usage.

Bryan Garner, in *Garner's Modern American Usage*, sums it up under the heading "The Pronoun Problem": "English has a number of common-sex general words, such as *person, anyone, everyone*, and *no one*, but it has no common-sex singular personal pronouns. Instead, we have *he, she*, and *it*. The traditional approach has been to use the masculine pronouns *he* and *him* to cover all people, male and female alike. That this practice has come under increasing attack has caused the most difficult problem in the realm of sexist language." As A. A. Milne wrote, "If the English language had been properly organised . . . there would be a word which meant both 'he' and 'she,' and I could write: 'If John or Mary comes, heesh will want to play tennis,' which would save a lot of trouble."

It certainly would. There have been numerous efforts to fix this defect of English. He-she and she-he, s/he and he/she and s/he/it are the least imaginative solutions. He/she, with a slash, is actually in the dictionary, dating to 1963. She/he is not; *Webster's* goes straight from "Sheetrock" to "sheikh," two potently masculine words. "She" contains "he," just as "woman" contains "man," but "he" doesn't like that: "she" ain't going nowhere without "he." "Heesh" has the lovely property of looking as if it had been formed when "she" backed into "he" and spun around. It's playful, as befits the creator of Winnie-the-Pooh and the sire of Christopher Robin.

The search has been on for a gender-neutral, or "epicene," pronoun in America since about 1850, when someone thought *ne, nis, nim* would do the job. Alternatives come from all over the alphabet. Gathered together, they look a little like the periodic table of elements. Where there are too many choices, there is often no single good one, and that is the case with the suggestions for a gender-neutral third-person-singular pronoun. There is *hse*, which is splendid and economical—a minimalist acronym—but unpronounceable. There are also *ip, ips* (1884) and *ha, hez, hem* (1927) and *shi, shis, shim* (1934) and *himorher* (which threatens to develop into *hemorrhoid*) (1935). Someone suggested we borrow *ta* and *ta-men* from the Mandarin (yeah, like that's going to happen). *Shem* and *herm* sound like Noah's offspring; *ho, hom, hos*, if they ever had a chance, would have succumbed to the "ho" problem; *se* and *hir* are apparently used by an online group devoted to sexual bondage; *ghach* is Klingon. And the search goes on. How about *mef* (male *e* female?). *Hu* is for human, *per* for person, *jee, jeir, jem* for God knows what, but they would be useful in Scrabble. *Ze* and *zon* sound German. Most of the others sound intergalactic.

Mary Orovan, a feminist poet, suggested *co, cos* in 1970, specifically for use in, say, documents addressing human rights. (At a ceremony honoring Susan B. Anthony, Orovan feminized the sign of the cross: "In the name of the Mother, the Daughter, and the Holy Granddaughter. Ah-women." Holy Mother Church may be feminine, but she's no feminist.) There is a scheme using *e, em,* and *eir* (1983), named for Michael Spivak. The Spivak pronouns build on the work of Christine M. Elverson, of Skokie, Illinois, who, in 1975, won a contest for best gender-neutral pronouns, run by a Chicago business organization. Her winning entry simply dropped the *th* from "they," "them," "their" to create *ey, em, eir.*

All these schemes are imposed. There is only one documented instance of a gender-neutral pronoun springing from actual speech, and that is "yo," which "spontaneously appeared in Baltimore city schools in the early-to-mid 2000s." "Peep yo" means "Get a load of her-or-him." "Yo" also has the added advantage of already belonging to the language, so it may actually have a chance. The people of Baltimore have spoken.

Perhaps the most ambitious—and ridiculous—scheme was suggested in 2014 by a law professor named C. Marshall Thatcher, who set forth in great detail an argument for *ee/eet.* As English is continually evolving and expanding, he says, building his case, it should be able to accommodate something as desperately needed as pronouns "that refer . . . to antecedents of the male gender, the female gender, or the neuter gender."

The grammarians would hop all over Thatcher before he even got started for confusing sex and gender: strictly speaking— very strictly speaking—the words "male" and "female" are nouns denoting sex, and "masculine" and "feminine" are adjectives meaning of or for men and women: feminine wiles, masculine bearing, etc. Furthermore, until recently "gender" was strictly a grammatical term. Fowler wrote, "To talk of *persons* or *creatures of the masculine* or *feminine g.,* meaning *of the male* or *female sex,* is either a jocularity (permissible or not according to context) or a blunder."

Thatcher declines his novel pronoun, beginning with the nominative *ee/eet* (he or she/he, she, or it). For the possessive, he proposes *hisers* (rhymes with "scissors"). ("Example: When a divorce decree awards marital property to one of the spouses, the property becomes hisers.") The objective (accusative) pronouns would be *herim* and *herimt*. ("'Herim' would rhyme with the first two syllables in the word 'perimeter'"—sounds like someone clearing hisers throat.) For skeptics, Thatcher points out that the Swedes invented a gender-neutral pronoun (*hen*) to use in preschools, to free children from gender stereotypes. And look at the success of the honorific "Ms.," he says.

But "Ms." is superficial, a title that you can click on when buying an airline ticket. Pronouns are deeply embedded in the language, and all these imposed schemes are doomed: the more logical they are, the more absurd the idea of putting them into practice. Rather than solve anything by blending in, the invented pronouns stand up and wave their arms around just when they should be disappearing.

Leaving aside invented or typographical solutions that look like Martian or borrow from the Chinese, Fowler sees three makeshift solutions for this deficiency in our language: We can use the so-called masculine rule, in which "he" is understood to stand for either the masculine or the feminine pronoun; we can use some form of "he or she, himself or herself," etc., however awkward; or we can resort to the non-gender-specific plural "their," which bends the number rule while finessing the gender. The first solution is the time-honored one. Male prescriptivists agree that "where the matter of sex is not conspicuous or important the masculine form shall be allowed to represent a person instead of a man, to say a man (homo) instead of a man (vir)." "Man" does have a dictionary definition that includes all humans, and it is just possible that the feminists have been literal-minded and, in pursuit of a political goal, have lost their sense of humor. It happens. *Homo* and *vir* are, of course, Latin, but even an ignoramus can infer their meanings from other English words: *homo* refers to the species (*Homo sapiens*); the meaning of *vir* is embodied in "virile"—capable of procreation, or (loosely) manly. But as Elaine Showalter, in that class on women in literature, pointed out, the rigid use of the masculine rule in, say, an article about menstruation or childbirth is absurd.

Despite its clunkiness, the second makeshift—the usage "he and she" in all its glorious declensions—has become common-place, so much so that this typo appeared in the *New York Times*, in a review by Dwight Garner of a book about aspiring writers: "The aspirant can then sink back into her or her individual slough of despond." One might view this as a victory for feminists, except that the context is so depressing, implying that women writers have a monopoly on the slough of despond. However widely the compound singular is adopted, to always have to write "he or she," "him or her," "his or hers" is pretty cumbersome.

Mostly, people have already thrown in their his-and-hers towels and turned to the third makeshift: the popular solution is to adopt the plural "their." The prescriptivists don't like it: Fowler calls it "the horrible *their*," and Bryan Garner sounds resigned as he writes, "Though the masculine singular personal pronoun may survive awhile longer as a generic term, it will probably be ultimately displaced by *they*, which is coming to be used alternatively as singular or plural." The descriptivists

come at it with a more upbeat attitude, citing the *OED*'s doc-
umentation of "their" in the Authorized Version of the Bible,
Shakespeare, Lewis Carroll, and Thackeray: "A person can't
help their birth," for example. As the easygoing David Marsh,
of the *Guardian*, says, "If they can do it, so can you. English,
after all, used to have a singular version of 'you'—*thee, thou* and
thy—and it is still heard in some dialects. . . . 'You' gradually
squeezed these words out to become standard for singular as
well as plural, and no great anguish seems to have been caused."
A sneaky way to justify the lack of concord between the plural
"they" and a singular antecedent is simply to relabel "they" as
singular. What such commentators do not mention is that in
almost every instance it's not the *writer* who is talking but a
character—it's dialogue, mostly in fiction, where anything can
happen. The Thackeray is Rosalind in *Vanity Fair*, talking about
Becky Thatcher: "'A person can't help their birth,' Rosalind
replied with great liberality."

I hate to say it, but the colloquial use of "their" when you mean
"his or her" is just wrong. It may solve the gender problem, and
there is no doubt that it has taken over in the spoken language,
but it does so at the expense of number. An antecedent that is in
the singular cannot take a plural pronoun. And yet it does, all
the time—certainly in speech. It's not fair. Why should a lowly
common-gender plural pronoun trump our singular feminine
and masculine pronouns, our kings and queens and jacks? If we
didn't make such a fuss about the epicene, the masculine pronoun
would just blend in and disappear: the invisible he. Working on a
piece by the television critic Emily Nussbaum, I noticed a "their"
with a singular antecedent and queried in "his," but Nussbaum
wanted no part of the patriarchal pronoun—"the invisible his"

was not invisible to her—and insisted on "his or her." I thought it stuck out, but it was her piece, so we did it her way.

It is best if these makeshift solutions don't draw attention to themselves, and we often try to rewrite a sentence to make the problem go away (although sometimes the copy editor herself must know when to go away). The longtime *New Yorker* staff writer Mark Singer used the vernacular "their" in a charming piece that read like a routine by a Borscht Belt comedian; his sentence would have had to be completely recast in order to avoid what Eleanor Gould called "number trouble." (Sounds a little like "female trouble.") What about "one's"? As an alternative, "one's" is so stiff that no one, not Fowler and certainly not Singer, seriously considers it. Singer wanted his language to reflect the way people talk, a not unreasonable expectation, and he was playing it for laughs. I backed down, allowing something ungrammatical to appear in the magazine, which, in future times, would be held up as proof that it was grammatical because *The New Yorker* had printed it. Oy vey! I have to admit that as a copy editor I agree with the conservatives—my job is to do no harm. But as a person—and as a writer and reader—I am all over the place. I admired both Nussbaum for finding a substitute for the natural-sounding plural and Singer for insisting on keeping it. Whatever they did, their pronouns ultimately blended in. And that's what you want.

Nobody seems to take very seriously a fourth possibility (fifth, counting *heesh* and its ilk): Why not mix it up a little? Why can't a woman use feminine pronouns if she feels like it? And what is stopping a man from once in a while throwing in a "her" or a "she"? Garner mentions it (*"as anybody can see for herself"*) but mostly to reject it or deride it as a gimmick resorted to by American academics for purposes of political correctness: "Such phrases are often alternated with those containing masculine pronouns, or, in some writing, appear uniformly. Whether this phraseology will someday stop sounding strange to most readers only time will tell." He warns that "the method carries two risks. First, unintended connotations may invade the writing." I am not sure what he means by this, but it sounds bitchy. "Second, this makeshift is likely to do a disservice to women in the long run, for it would probably be adopted by only a small minority of writers: the rest would continue with the generic masculine pronoun." The force of Garner's colon there suggests that those who continue to use the generic masculine pronoun will do so with a vengeance, perhaps in boldface, as if to strengthen the masculine grip on the language, which would amount to a fresh insult to womankind.

Yet the "small minority of writers" includes David Foster Wallace, who happens to be one of Garner's favorites. And the effect of that feminine pronoun, at least on me, is to engender sympathy. I like better any male writer who is uxorious in his use of pronouns. Sing in me, o Muse, of that small minority of men who are secure enough in their masculinity to use the feminine third-person singular!

———

It's possible that the makeshifts come more easily to me because I have experienced a pronoun transplant. Nothing makes it clearer how intimately and deeply pronouns are embedded in our lives than having to alter them to refer to someone you've known all your life. Just when I was mounting an assault on the Italian language, sorting the nouns that ended in *a* (mostly feminine) from the nouns that ended in *o* (mostly masculine), struggling to make sense of the ones that ended in *e*, the difference between sex and gender leaped out of the textbook and into my real life: my younger brother announced that he was transsexual. Dee was two years younger than me, and we had been close—or at least *I* thought we were close. We grew up together in Cleveland and we both escaped to New York, where we were friends, sometimes neighbors, often confidantes, collaborators, drinking buddies.

I am grateful for the word "sibling," stiff as it is. Not every language has an epicene word for brother or sister. Ancient Greek had a word that meant essentially "womb-mate," but Italian has only *il fratello* and *la sorella*, and no way to describe a transsexual sibling unless you fiddle with the inflections: *il sorello, la fratella, la fratello/sorella, il sorello/fratella*. One of the first sentences I formed in Italian class was "*Mio fratello vuole essere mia sorella*": "My brother wants to be my sister."

What is the first thing everyone wants to know when a baby is born? Girl or boy, right? What is more basic to your identity than that? Growing up, I was very well aware that my brother was a boy; I defined myself in relation to him, and it was my observation that he got much better treatment than I did. He never had to do the dishes or polish the tiles around the fake fireplace, and when he grew up he wouldn't have to wear a girdle every day of his life, the way our mother did. I was jealous of him, fairy-tale jealous, and in my older sister's way I coveted everything he had. That's right, everything. I had no pride in being a girl. So when, as an adult, my brother announced his intention to become the girl he had always wanted to be—to have a masculine body revised to reflect a feminine soul—I felt threatened and betrayed.

The idea that gender in language is decorative, a way of dressing up words, can be applied to the human body: things that identify us outwardly as male or female—breasts, hips, bulges— are decorative as well as essential to the survival of the species. Lipstick and high heels are inflections, tokens of the feminine: lures, sex apps. Those extra letters dangling at the ends of words are the genitalia of grammar. And the pronouns turn out to be in our marrow.

Before long, my sibling and I were engaged in a pronoun war. It started in Cleveland, where we had gone to watch out for our father in the nursing home while our mother was in Oregon, spending Christmas with our older brother and his family. The first day there, before going to visit Dad in the nursing home, Dee came downstairs wearing lipstick and blush. "Too much makeup for nine o'clock in the morning," I said. Dee wanted to go shopping while we were in Cleveland, and told me that shoes are particularly hard for a male-to-female transsexual. I remembered a shoe store for big and tall girls downtown in the arcade and found it in the phonebook: Mar-Lou Tall Girls Shoe Shop, and we went downtown together. The saleslady seemed to think I was Dee's mother. "He wants some ladies' shoes," I said, aware that I had already stuck my foot in my mouth. But Dee, who was munching on a bag of roasted cashews, did not react. She picked out a pair of low black leather bootlike shoes with buckles, a pair of brown oxfords with thick treads (it was important to have shoes that worked both ways), and some slip-ons, which even I had to admit were surprisingly becoming. He/she carried them proudly in a Mar-Lou Tall Girls Shoe Shop bag. To celebrate, we went to a bar—an old favorite, Otto Moser's, that used to be decorated with vintage photos of vaudeville days and served beer in thick goblets called fishbowls. Dee's thrill over the new shoes was something I could appreciate—every girl loves new shoes—and I found it poignant that Dee had never before had a pair of shoes that could be kicked off, like slippers.

We were in Cleveland for about a week, and Dee spent the days combing the thrift shops and coming back with bags and bags of ladies' clothing. The bed was heaped with sweaters featuring eccentric sleeves and striking necklines, scarves, even a feather boa. Dee changed clothes several times a day and experimented with hair and makeup. I got ornery waiting outside the bathroom while Dee was in there primping—my own gender inflections were confined to the most conservative possible expressions of femininity: I used Chapstick and wore earrings that looked like buckshot—and I'd do a double take in my mother's kitchen when my sibling appeared in a top that emphasized his/her new little boobs, and the lipstick stains on the glasses that *I* had to wash really pissed me off. Dee was like a deranged fourteen-year-old.

The tension grew to the point where Dee said, "I'm thinking of flying home." I didn't want that. "This is my vacation," Dee explained. "It's my chance to come out of the closet, to experiment. It's important to wear makeup in order to let people know that I, at least, think I'm a woman. And you're *so mean.*" At one point, in the car, when Dee had taken out a little pot of lip gloss and a brush to apply a fresh coat while I was backing out the driveway, I slammed on the brakes. I thought it was funny.

I felt bad and said I would try to do better. Our mother was coming home that night, and Dee was nervous. "It'll be the first time I see Mom," Dee said. Actually, it was the first time Mom would be seeing *Dee,* but I didn't say anything. To mark our truce, we went out to dinner at the Great Lakes Brewing Company. It was crowded, and we had to stand in the bar area until a table was available. In the old days, it was easy to be in a bar with my brother; I just stood there and he went to the bar and got drinks for both of us. But now I became aware that I was no longer with my brother. This person thought he was a woman. I tried seeing Dee as a woman: Tall, deep-set eyes, narrow face. Kind of ragged eyebrows and terrible teeth, but those things could be taken care of. A delicate face, with a fine complexion. My complexion. Our mother's complexion.

Finally, we got a table and ordered, and I was chattering away, feeling relieved in spite of myself, when the waiter arrived with our order. "Cheeseburger?" he said.

"That's his," I said, and picked up my fork and started to renew the conversation. But something was amiss. Dee seemed to have no appetite. "What's wrong?" I asked. Maybe the waiter had forgotten the sliced raw onion. Dee looked away. Were those tears? What was there to cry about?

"It feels so hopeless," Dee said. "You say 'That's his' and don't even know you've said it."

I was aghast. I had thought we were getting along, and a mere pronoun had landed like a cannonball between us. I couldn't believe I was going to have to change my pronouns—words I had used confidently since childhood. I could never say "he" or "him" or "his" without driving my sibling to despair? It was like speaking a foreign language, always having to think ahead to the next bit of gender. Even when I saw how it hurt Dee's feelings if I referred to her as him, it took a huge effort to get the pronoun out right.

Maybe the waiter did think Dee was a woman, and with a single thoughtless word I had stomped on her dream. To me, at the time, it *was* a dream. I didn't think anyone would ever seriously take Dee as a woman. But gradually Dee pulled it off. "Ladies!" the host would greet us when we walked into a restaurant. At first I thought that everyone had been hoodwinked, but in the end it was I who saw someone who wasn't there.

Mom came home that night. She was very sweet to Dee. In the morning, while Dee was taking her time in the bathroom (our drive through Pennsylvania would call for full evening makeup), I went out for doughnuts. "You look nice," Mom said to Dee when she came downstairs. They talked clothes a little, which thrilled Dee—she was dying to talk girl talk with some female member of the family. Mom said, "I wish I could see all your new things"— Dee's thrift-store buys were packed in two huge Hefty bags—but I was all for hustling us out the door. It was New Year's Eve, and I was going to have to drive Dee through Manhattan, all the way to her door, with her new wardrobe. Mom even admired the shoes: "They make your feet look smaller." It was just what Dee wanted to hear.

"He looks kind of cute, doesn't he?" Mom said to me.

"She," I said, as Dee beamed. "*She* looks kind of cute."

Chapter 4
....

BETWEEN YOU AND ME

W HEN I WAS IN GRADUATE SCHOOL, living on my own in
the Vermont countryside, I decided I should learn how cars
worked. I wanted to be self-reliant. I drove a '65 Plymouth Fury
II, in dark blue-green. It had a huge expanse of windshield, which
was great for scenic drives and winter sunsets, and a V-8 engine,
which meant nothing to me. I knew how to pump gas and check
the oil and change a flat tire, but that was about it. My father had
discouraged me from learning anything about the workings of
the internal-combustion engine. When I said I wanted to learn
how cars worked, he said, "It's easy. I'll tell you everything you
need to know. You put the key in the ignition and you turn it."

Thanks, Dad. To his credit, he had also advised me to cultivate
a mechanic at a local gas station. But out in the country there were
no gas stations—just a pump at Marble's Store, where you could
leave the keys in the car and Marble would move it if it was in the

way. So I registered for an adult-education class in auto mechanics one night a week at the local high school. On the first night, the auto-mechanics teacher used a word I had never understood the meaning of: "gasket." I had blown one once, on a friend's car, driving too fast on hair-raising canyon roads in Utah, and I knew that it cost a lot to replace, and the car was never the same. (Sorry!) Now, at last, I was going to find out what a gasket was. So I raised my hand and asked, "What's a gasket?" The teacher, who looked like a used-car salesman, defined "gasket" by using three other words that I didn't know the meaning of: "crankcase," "pistons," "carburetor" . . . I'm still not sure what a gasket is.

Grammar also has some intimidating terms, and grammarians throw them around constantly, but you don't need to know them in order to use the language ("You put the key in the ignition and you turn it"). E. B. White admitted that before working on *The Elements of Style* he was the kind of writer who did not have "any exact notion of what is taking place under the hood." To understand how the language works, though—to master the mechanics of it—you have to roll up your sleeves and join the ink-stained wretches as we name the parts, being careful to define them in a way that makes them simpler instead of more complicated, and see how they work together. Bear with me while I find the little hook that holds the hood in place and prop it open with this stick. I am going to attempt to diagnose one of the most barbaric habits in contemporary usage.

———

Just between you and me, I suffer, and the whole body of the English language shudders, when, say, a shoe salesman trying

to gain my trust leans forward and says, "Between you and I
. . ." Or when a character in a movie complains to a girl that "it's
just not right, lumping you and I together," or when the win-
ner of the Academy Award for best actress thanks a friend "for
getting Sally and I together." Maybe it's the heat of the moment:
maybe people think "me" might be OK at home, where you can
afford to be a bit vulgar, but it can't possibly be right in a formal
setting.

Sticklers have been complaining about this for centuries, but
we'll go back only to Dwight Macdonald, who, in his 1961 essay
on *Webster's Third*, referred to "between you and I" as a wide-
spread and well-known solecism. ("Solecism" is a fancy word
for mistake; it refers especially to mistakes in usage that betray
the user's pomposity and ignorance.) David Foster Wallace lists
"between you and I" second in a catalogue of blunders that pref-
aces his essay "Authority and American Usage," a review of *Garner's Modern American Usage*. Wallace was a fabulous stickler—a
snoot, in his own term. (His mother was an English teacher.)
Fortunately, he had the gift of writing cutting-edge prose with
exquisite propriety, and so he makes it OK to care about such
things. Garner himself devotes a column and a half to "between
you and I," noting that this is a grammatical error "committed
almost exclusively by educated speakers trying a little too hard
to sound refined but stumbling badly."

This kind of thing occurs all the time. On an old episode
of *The Honeymooners*, Ralph Kramden has jilted Ed Norton and
found another bowling partner, and says to Norton, "We have
already reserved that alley for Teddy and I." Ralph is trying to
show his superiority. He's not the most articulate guy (*humminna-
humminna-humminna-humminna*), but by putting the other per-

son first—"you," Sally, Teddy—he and the others have let word
order trick them into using the wrong pronoun.

First, let us praise the impulse behind all these slips—the
salesman and the emotionally damaged son (or the scriptwriter)
and the movie star are all humbling themselves by putting
another person first. Then let us gently point out that if they
were not so fucking polite, if they occasionally put themselves
first, they would know they had it wrong. No one would begin
a confidence with "Between I and you," or complain because
someone was "lumping I and you together," or thank a friend
"for getting I and Sally together." Even Ralph Kramden would
probably not say, "We have already reserved that alley for I
and Teddy," although it sounds very grand. But if you go ahead
and put yourself first, using "me" instead of "I," you can hear
that "me" is right—"between me and you," "lumping me and you
together," "getting me and Sally together"—and if you still think
it's impolite and your mother or first-grade teacher would dis-
approve, move "me" to the other end and you have good grammar and etiquette, too: "Between you and me," "lumping you and
me together," thanks "for getting Sally and me together." In the
case of Ralph Kramden, the immortal bus driver of Bensonhurst,
"reserving an alley for Teddy and I" is fine, because Jackie Glea-
son was a comedian, and the more ridiculous he makes his character sound, the better. It's funnier with the mistake, and also
revealing of Ralph's wounded pride and his need to feel superior,
to show that he is more refined than Norton. It also exposes his
ignorance to us, the viewers, and makes us feel superior. It's a
pratfall in dialogue form.

It comes up at home and at work (where it shouldn't), on real
vacations and on busman's holidays. A couple I'll call Penny and

Jeter come out to my bungalow in Rockaway and proceed to devour the cherries I've put out in a bowl on the table. Jeter says, "Don't put a bowl of cherries in front of Penny and I." I am happy that I bought something they like—I like cherries, too—and I'm not about to snatch the cherries away unless Jeter learns to say "in front of Penny and me." In fact I find his uxoriousness charming—he is showing great sensitivity to his wife. But I do register unease at his locution, and I might think twice about buying cherries the next time.

Someone at work sends an e-mail to the whole editorial staff that says, "If you have a copy of Tom Vanderbilt's *Traffic,* please contact Vicky or I." "Vicky or me!" I mutter at my computer. "You should know better! You would never say, 'Please contact I.'" I don't actually say anything to the offender, but I'm not lending him my copy of *Traffic,* either. To my surprise, one of his underlings shoots back a reply-all e-mail, correcting her boss: "Vicky or *me.*" I wonder if she will get promoted or overlooked the next time there's an opening for assistant boss. My friend Lucette, one of a pair of lovely confident literary sisters for whom I have the utmost respect, has spoken deferentially all her life of her and her sister as "Kate and I." They are the most loyal, supportive sisters ever. When Lucette transposes "Kate and I" into prepositional phrases, saying things like "He sent flowers to Kate and I," some lining between my skin and my inner organs begins to shrink. Just once, I murmured "Kate and *me*"—she is, after all, the chairman of the English department at a world-class university, and I wouldn't want her to be embarrassed—and she responded, "Dialogue!" It's true that all these examples are from speech or e-mail—nobody was videotaping our conversation or chiseling it in stone. Furthermore, the linguists are on her side. They say that "Kate and I," "Vicky and I," "Penny and I" are units, and people tend to keep them invariable, even when their function in the sentence dictates that they be changed to "Kate and me," "Vicky and me," "Penny and me." They treat these compounds as if there were quotation marks around them, like "The King and I." I loved *The King and I,* especially Yul Brynner and Deborah Kerr doing "Shall We Dance" (though, between you and me, I could do without "Getting to Know You").

My friend Diane started a Facebook conversation after her son said to her, "That's what they did for Nolan and I." "Nolan and ME," she said. Her son, she wrote, argued that "the language has evolved, and today many people would think 'Nolan and me' was actually wrong." Then he added the sinker, as in sinker of hearts in the chests of the parental units: "Besides, who cares?"

There was a chorus of "me"s (they were her Facebook friends, after all), but a handful of responders agreed with her son that language evolves and suggested that "you and me" may be going the way of "I and thou." Diane gave a further example: "Last summer, I was looking for my sunglasses, and said, about a pair Jamie was holding, 'Are those they?' He answered, 'No, those are not they,' and then burst out laughing."

Or think of the song "The Girl from Ipanema." I don't know the lyrics in Portuguese (it's Brazilian, of course), but this gentle bossa nova, in the famous English version sung by Astrud Gilberto, has a pronoun in it that I've always found distracting. A man watches a beautiful girl pass daily on her way to the sea; he loves her, but "she looks straight ahead—not at he." Yowch. What went wrong here? Can't a stickler kick back with a caipirinha for a little easy listening? Many more people have enjoyed the song than have gritted their teeth over it. I asked a linguist, and she said, "I always thought it was a joke." It turns out that someone else who gritted his teeth over it was Norman Gimbel, the author of the English version, who had written, "She looks straight ahead, not at *me*." It was the singer who substituted the "he," perhaps in an attempt to adjust the lyrics to her own gender (the song was written to be sung by a man, after all), and without total mastery of English. At any rate, the consensus seems to be that nothing, but nothing, can diminish the charms of the girl from Ipanema.

"Those are they" or "not at he" might make some people smile, but I keep wondering: Why *do* we care? Is it just what we're used to? Are we protecting our delicate sensibilities? You can't even warn kids that unless they get their pronouns straight they can't grow up to be president, because our most eloquent president in decades, Barack Obama, says things like "a very personal decision for Michelle and I" or "graciously invited Michelle and I." I got excited when I read this passage in *Gone Girl*, by Gillian Flynn: "The woman remained in the car the whole time, a pacifiered toddler in her arms, watching her husband and me trade cash for keys. (That is the correct grammar, you know: her husband and me.)" Way to go, Gillian Flynn! I thought. May you sell as many billions of books as McDonald's sells burgers! Later I realized that it was the character's thought, not the author's (although it may also be hers), and the character turned out to be just the sort of uptight entitled snob who gives good grammar a bad name.

So it may be quixotic of me, the battle may well have long been lost, but I am going to "requeft once for all," as Noah Webster would say, "that it may be attended to." Why exactly is "between you and me" correct, and "between you and I" wrong? Sometimes if you take your time and sort out the parts of speech and learn the pattern of the grammar, and see the beauty and the economy of it, you'll find it easier to nail the usage.

———

We're going to start with the verb "to be," move to the transitive verbs, take on the nouns that come before and after the verbs, and tinker with the prepositions attached to the nouns and verbs: it's all about function in a sentence. This is applied mechanics.

The most important verb is the verb "to be" in all its glory: am, are, is, was, were, will be, has been. Grammarians know it as the copulative verb. (Many grammarians prefer "linking verb," but I have to say that the term "copulative verb" impressed me when I heard it for the first time, in a linguistics course during my junior year of college. It was my first inkling that English grammar could be interesting.) The function of the copulative verb is to fit nouns together, to conjoin them as a plumber fits pipes, screwing the male into the female (these are actual terms from plumbing), to make the two one. The copulative verb functions almost as an equal sign: "I am a copy editor." "My plumber is a saint." "You are the reader."

The nouns and pronouns in those simple sentences (I, you, copy editor, plumber, saint, reader) all fall into the same grammatical category. In grammar, the role that a noun (or its avatar the mighty pronoun) plays in the sentence is called its "case." The noun that is the subject (I, my plumber, you) is in the subjective case and the noun that it links to (copy editor, saint, reader) through the verb is also in the subjective case. That is the power of the copulative verb. (I get so mad when the verb "is" or "be" is left lowercase in a title. Just because it's small doesn't mean it's not important!) The Latinate term for subjective is nominative, which is easy even if you don't know Latin, because to nominate, in English, is to name and a noun is always the name of something. But not all verbs can be the verb "to be" (although there are some that behave the same way), and nouns don't always stay in the subjective case. It all depends on the model of the sentence.

There is something called a transitive verb. The word "transitive" leaves me cold. I wish there were another word for it. It is from the Latin, but don't panic. We know enough English words with Latin roots to infer that *trans* means "across" or "through," as in "transmit" (to put across) or "translucent" (allowing light to go through); the Central Park transverse carries you through or across Central Park. This kind of verb transfers (bears across) some kind of activity from the subject to another noun, not so closely identified with the subject, called the object. "The mechanic inspects the car." "The car fails inspection." "The engine needs oil." The transitive verb points forward to something, to whatever will fulfill it. What object did the mechanic inspect? The car. What did the car fail? The inspection. What does the engine need? Oil. These nouns are direct objects of the verbs, and when a noun functions as an object it is in the objective case. The Latin for this is "accusative," as in "I accused the mechanic of overcharging me." "Accusative" is a word you see a lot of if you study a foreign language, which I recommend. I never learned any of this stuff until I studied German in my senior year of college.

Why am I telling you this? Because other languages, including German, Greek, and Latin, have the accusative case, and in some of these languages (notably Greek, German, Latin, and Irish) nouns take a different form depending on whether they are subjects or objects. Grammarians call these forms inflections. Also, some other languages have three, four, five, seven, fifteen different cases, and not just the nouns but everything that goes with them—articles, adjectives—has to be inflected to match. In English, we are mostly spared this bother. Only the pronouns, our ancient, venerable pronouns, are inflected in ways that link us to the Anglo-Saxons. Moreover, because our pronouns behave in some of the same ways that nouns and pronouns behave in other languages, the case system connects English to other languages—to Portuguese and Dutch and Latin and ancient Greek—making us a part of global history.

We learn, stumblingly, as children how to inflect pronouns. "Her is a sweetheart" is perfectly good baby talk. I have a friend in Queens who says things like "Me and him are going away for the weekend." Good for her! This is not what I am trying to correct. I am not trying to fit anyone for a linguistic straitjacket. Strictly speaking, the copulative verb calls for the nominative case in the predicate. The subjective, or nominative, pronouns are: I, you, he/she/it, we, you, they. So the child eventually learns to say of his little sister, "She is a sweetheart" (probably by that time he doesn't think so anymore, though). Helen Stark, my boss in the editorial library, calling her husband, Ira, from work, would announce herself by saying, "Hi, it's I." This shows what stern stuff Helen was made of. When my friend Diane was looking for her sunglasses and phrased her question "Are those they?," it may have made her son laugh, but it would have gladdened the hearts of her teachers at Brearley. And when Mr. Burns, on *The Simpsons*, finds out that Homer's father, Abe Simpson, used to wrestle under the name Raging Abe, and shouts "You were he!" his excellent grammar marks him as a villain.

By the way, there are verbs that do not take an object and are not copulative. Intransitive verbs reflect back on the subject. While a transitive verb directs the action of the subject onto an object, the intransitive verb expresses some action purely of the subject itself: "Humpty Dumpty sat on the wall." "The self-driving car took off by itself." "The little dog laughed to see such a sight." The copulative verb is an intransitive verb (it doesn't take an object) that belongs to a special high-performance category. In *The Transitive Vampire*, Karen Elizabeth Gordon supplies a list of copulative verbs: in addition to forms of the verb "to be," they include "verbs of the senses (*look, hear, taste, smell, sound*); and verbs like *appear, seem, become, grow, prove, remain*." It is because these verbs are copulative and not merely intransitive that we say something "tastes good" (an adjective), not "well" (an adverb): the verb is throwing the meaning back onto the noun, and nouns are modified by adjectives, not adverbs. It's "I felt bad," not "I felt badly," because "to feel badly" would mean "to grope about ineptly." The verb "felt"—definitely a verb of the senses, though not on Gordon's list—fuses the "bad" to the subject, rather than simply using an adverb to modify itself.

One might reasonably ask, if we can use the objective for the subjective, as in "It's me again," why can't we use the subjective for the objective? Grammar is a little like a plumbing system. Some systems are designed to dispose of two-ply toilet paper. Others are more delicate and are designed with the capacity for one-ply. You can flush one-ply in a system built for two-ply, but if you force two-ply into a system that tolerates only one-ply, you're asking for trouble.

It's an interesting mistake, I'll say that. It's as if people thought that the nominative pronouns were more formal—as if

English had separate forms for "I" and "me" the way Italian and French and German have separate forms of "you" for familiar and formal. "I" is not a formal version of "me." "Me" does sound more intimate somehow—maybe it's this confidential air that someone speaking in public wants to avoid. "I," "he," "she," "we," "they" are stiffer than their counterparts in the objective case. "Me," "him," "her," "us," "them" are softer, more malleable; they go in places more easily. Maybe it's something to do with being objects, borne along, instead of bold subjects, which take responsibility for their actions. Maybe it would help if people practiced, like singers vocalizing: Between you and *mi-mi-mi-mi-mi.*

If you prefer an automotive explanation, try this: The head gasket, as I understand it, is a kind of seal, keeping the oil that lubricates the engine out of the car part (carburetor? crankcase? How about solenoid?) where the fuel mixes with oxygen in just the right proportions to fire the pistons that keep the motor running and the car on the road. The pronouns are the grease. The verbs are the gasoline and the nouns are the air. The case system is the gasket that keeps everything running smoothly. You notice it only when someone blows it. And if that doesn't work for you, just put the key in the ignition and turn it.

———

Once you know about the nominative and the accusative cases, and have a firm grasp on the copulative verb, another frequent usage issue becomes as easy as a glide in a gondola: the distinction between "who" and "whom." This one troubles many of us, though there are some who think it's not worth worrying about at all. "The *who/whom* distinction," Steven Pinker writes, "is on the way out; in the United States, *whom* is used consistently only by careful writers and pretentious speakers." I don't think anyone would argue with that. David Marsh, the style editor of the *Guardian*, titled his usage book *For Who the Bell Tolls*; the cover illustration shows the *m* being rubbed out of John Donne's famous line. "Whom" may indeed be on the way out, but so is Venice, and we still like to go there.

Is there ever a time when "whom" is right, outside of "For whom the bell tolls"? And how does it work when it's right? "For whom the bell tolls" is a direct object in the poem: "And therefore never send to know for whom the bell tolls." It answers the question "what?" Never send to know what? But in this case "whom" is simply the object of the preposition "for": the bell tolls for whom? Those are five of the most loaded words in the English language.

"Who" is used when the pronoun is the subject or a predicate nominative, and "whom" when it's a direct object, an indirect object, or the object of a preposition. There is one snag: Sometimes an object is not just a noun but a clause, which is like a sentence within the sentence, and has a subject, verb, and object of its own. When that happens, don't panic. Ship your oars for a moment and drift until you figure it out.

Here is a prosaic example of a construction that came close to going to press with "who": "the dissident blogger, whom the government had recently allowed to travel outside of the country." If you recast the clause as its own sentence and change the relative pronoun to a personal pronoun, its case will be apparent. The government had recently allowed *her* (objective) to travel outside of the country.

And here is a "whom" that should have been a "who," from

C&T (*Car & Travel*), the magazine I get in the mail from AAA, the automobile association: "If someone approaches you waving a big pair of greasy jumper cables, tell him that you've contacted your roadside service provider and the police, whom will be there shortly." Who will be there shortly? The police will be there shortly. The police is the subject of the clause, so the relative pronoun stays in the nominative.

Cyberspace is awash in "whom"s that should be "who"s, and many of them are negligible—you look at them once, wince, and it's over—but others linger, because the sentences they are embedded in are otherwise delightful, and you'd like to see them enjoying their instant on your Facebook feed. I know that my friend Little Annie Bandez will forgive me for using as examples some of the heartfelt wise-ass things she has posted. Annie wrote, "In this bright fall light the damage humans be wearing is so in your face that its near impossible to not love—even those whom are screaming for a bitch slap."

Annie is right to think that the object of her love should logically be in the objective case and that the objective of "who" is "whom"; however, she has cast the object not as a simple pronoun (there is an implied "them" following "impossible not to love") but as a hilariously provocative clause: "those [humans]" is the subject and "are screaming" is the verb and "for a bitch slap" is a prepositional phrase describing what they are screaming for. Because "those humans" are doing the screaming, they are the subject of the clause, and the pronoun should be in the nominative, even though the humans in need of slapping are filling the role of the sentence's object. Ask yourself, who is screaming for a bitch slap? The answer is "they" are, the nominative pronoun, so "who" should be in the nominative case.

"Some public display of affection photos remind me of 'Best In Show' owners walking their dogs—except the relationship between one and their pet children is true— Sometimes some human PDAs really skeeve me out . . . the goo goo eye ones where ya can tell whom is top dog- oy vey maria Im cranky today"

Bitch, you be even crankier when you see this. I love the verb "skeeve," and I get that "PDA" means "public display of affection" (though at first I thought it was a venereal disease), and I can do without hyphens in "the goo goo eye ones" but, again, the object of "ya can tell"—what can you tell?—is a clause, practically a sentence in itself: "who is top dog?"

I love the gritty sentiment behind these updates, but the effect is undercut for me by the grammar error sticking up like a chunk of flotsam in midstream. Here's the takeaway: "who" does not change to "whom" just because it is in the middle of the sentence. The choice of "who" or "whom" is governed not by its role as the object of the sentence or the object of a preposition but by its role in the group of words that has been plugged into that position. Break it down: You can tell he (or she) is top dog. You would never say, "You can tell him (or her) is top dog." That's the point: "who" and "whom" are standing in for a pronoun: "who" stands in for "he, she, they, I, we"; "whom" stands in for "him, her, them, me, us."

Incidentally, all of this applies more to written language than to spoken language. In spoken language, don't take any chances: unless you are really sure where you're going, use who (or whoever). And remember: "Who" does not change to "whom" just because it's in the middle of the sentence.

The correct use of "whom" is easier than you think. When it is right, it is sublime. When it is wrong, it blocks your passage.

Chapter 5
....

COMMA COMMA COMMA COMMA, CHAMELEON

THE COMMA WAS INVENTED BY Aldo Manuzio, a printer working in Venice, circa 1490. It was intended to prevent confusion by separating things. In the Greek, *komma* means "something cut off," a segment. (Aldo was printing Greek classics during the High Renaissance. The comma was a Renaissance invention.) As the comma proliferated, it started generating confusion. Basically, there are two schools of thought: One plays by ear, using the comma to mark a pause, like dynamics in music; if you were reading aloud, the comma would suggest when to take a breath. The other uses punctuation to clarify the meaning of a sentence by illuminating its underlying structure. Each school believes that the other gets carried away. It can be tense and kind of silly, like the argument among theologians about how many angels can fit on the head of a pin. How many commas can fit into a sentence by Herman Melville? Or, closer to home, into a sentence from *The New Yorker?*

Even something as ostensibly simple as the serial comma can arouse strong feelings. The serial comma is the one before "and" in a series of three or more things. With the serial comma: My favorite cereals are Cheerios, Raisin Bran, and Shredded Wheat. Without the serial comma: I used to like Kix, Trix and Wheat Chex. (Question: Why, if there is alphabet soup, do we not have punctuation cereal? Would it be so hard to develop a high-fiber cereal comma that retained its shape in milk?) Proponents of the serial comma say that it is preferable because it prevents ambiguity, and I'll go along with that. Also, I'm lazy, and I find it easier to use the serial comma consistently rather than stop every time I come to a series and register whether or not the comma before the "and" preceding the last item is actually preventing ambiguity. Pressed to come up with an example of a series that was unambiguously ambiguous without the serial comma, I couldn't think of a good one. An ambiguous series proved so elusive that I wondered whether perhaps we could do without the serial comma after all. In my office, this is heresy, but I will say it anyway and risk being burned at the stake: Isn't the "and" sufficient? After all, that's what the other commas in a series stand for: "Lions and tigers and bears, oh my!" A comma preceding "and" is redundant. I was a comma apostate.

Fortunately, the Internet is busy with examples of series that are absurd without the serial comma:

"We invited the strippers, JFK and Stalin."

(This has been illustrated online, and formed the basis of a two-part poll: for or against the serial comma, and which stripper had the better outfit, JFK or Stalin. The serial comma and Stalin won.)

"This book is dedicated to my parents, Ayn Rand and God."

(Also widely quoted; variations on God's mate include Hillary Clinton.)

And there was the country-and-western singer who "was joined by his two ex-wives, Kris Kristofferson and Waylon Jennings."

The bottom line is to choose one and be consistent and try not to make a moral issue out of it. Or is it? Maybe it's better to judge each series on its merits, applying the serial comma where it's needed and suppressing it where it's not. Many newspapers, both American and British, do not use the serial comma, which underscores the idea that the news is meant to be read fast, in the dead-tree version or on the screen, because it's not news for long. It's ephemeral. Print—or, rather, text—should be streamlined and unencumbered. Maybe the day is coming when the newsfeed-style three dots (ellipsis) between items, like the eternal ribbon of news circling the building at One Times Square or the CNN crawl, will dominate, and all text will look like Céline. Certainly advertising—billboards, road signs, neon—repels punctuation. Leaving out the serial comma saves time and space. The editors of *Webster's Third* saved eighty pages by cutting down on commas.

But suppose you're not in a hurry. Suppose you move your lips when you read, or pronounce every word aloud in your head, and you're reading a Victorian novel or a history of Venice. You have plenty of time to crunch commas. If I worked for a publication that did not use the serial comma, I would adjust— convert from orthodox to reformed—but for now I remain loyal to the serial comma, because it actually does sometimes prevent ambiguity and because I've gotten used to the way it looks. It gives starch to the prose, and can be very effective. If a sentence were a picket fence, the serial commas would be posts at regular intervals.

I feel my hackles rise, however, when I hear people refer to the serial comma as the Oxford comma. Why does Oxford get all the credit? Why does the stricter, more conservative choice belong to the university that gave us the eponymous shirt with the button-down collar and the androgynous lace-up shoe? Why not the Harvard comma, or the Rutgers comma, or the Cornhusker comma? I went up to Oxford once—or do I mean down? It was on a day trip from London, and I had a look at the cottage gardens and stopped in a pub for lunch—thatched roofs, separate entrances for ladies and for farm workers—and I don't know when I've felt so alienated.

The Oxford comma refers to the Oxford University Press, whose house style is to use the serial comma. (The public-relations department at Oxford doesn't use it, however. Presumably PR people see it as a waste of time and space. The business end of these operations is always in a hurry and does not approve of clutter. The serial comma is a pawn in the war between town and gown.) To call it the Oxford comma gives it a bit of class, a little snob appeal. Kids use it (or, rather, "reference" it) on their Twitter bios and their match.com profiles to show that they have standards. Chances are that if you use the Oxford comma you brush the crumbs off your shirtfront before going out. The British get to have it both ways: they deride us Americans for our allegiance to a comma that they named and then rejected as pretentious.

Charles Dickens is a prime example of a writer who punctuates by ear. Dickens was famous during his lifetime for the readings he gave from his work, and I suspect that an enterprising forensic scholar, using Dickens's commas as a guide, could develop equipment that would measure the author's lung capacity by having an actor read aloud from his books. We know that Dickens got paid by the word (writers still do), a fact that is often used to explain his prodigious output, but I think he might have collected a bonus for punctuation. Dickens was especially fond of inserting a comma between the subject and the predicate, one of the few things that the two modern schools of punctuation agree is a mistake. You can barely read two pages of Dickens without being stopped by something like this, from *Nicholas Nickleby*: "But what principally attracted the attention of Nicholas, was the old gentleman's eye. . . . Grafted upon the quaintness and oddity of his appearance, was something so indescribably engaging . . ."

By modern standards, these thudding commas are offenses for which Dickens ought to be sent to study with Mr. Squeers. They are no doubt intended to give a lift to the voice, a pause as the writer, reading aloud (if only inside the reader's head), injects a bit of suspense. "The first house to which they bent their steps, was situated in a terrace of respectable appearance." I know it was the fashion then—but so were bustles. These big-ass commas are often inserted between the verb and the object as well. The following is from a letter that Dickens wrote in 1856: "She brought me for a present, the most hideous Ostrich's Egg ever laid." Because of the comma, the sentence actually begins to misread as if the pronoun were the direct object—

"She brought *me* for a present"—before resolving itself into the true direct object: "the most hideous Ostrich's Egg ever laid." Obviously, none of this is meant to suggest that Dickens is overrated. His commas are a matter of historical record, and so much of Dickens is dialogue. And tempted as I might be to mess with Dickens's commas if I were copy-editing him (which would be a great pleasure), I don't let them interfere with my enjoyment of, say, Mr. Boffin, in *Our Mutual Friend*, or the Infant Phenomenon, in *Nicholas Nickleby*. I can't help but think that the way we punctuate now is the right way—that we are living in a punctuation renaissance—and we can at least learn from Dickens not to abuse the comma by using it to separate the subject from the verb or the verb from the object.

Since its invention, punctuation has grown and developed and been subjected to various theories and practices, like medicine or millinery. Herman Melville was either a spectacularly ham-handed punctuator or a victim of the copy-editing conventions of his time. Or both. Here is an example from *White-Jacket; or, The World in a Man-of-War*, first published in 1850:

"Often I have lain thus, when the fact, that if I laid much longer I would actually freeze to death, would come over me with such overpowering force as to break the icy spell, and starting to my feet, I would endeavour to go through the combined manual and pedal exercise to restore the circulation."

There are plenty of funky things going on in this sentence. Why would Melville break up the phrase "the fact that"? He often puts a comma before "that." It's tempting to think that he had it mixed up with "which." Melville was punctuating for cadence, giving suggestions for how to read aloud, but his commas, by modern standards, are more like obstacles than aids to reading, and provide excellent material for deconstruction.

One test for whether you need commas to set off a group of words is to see whether the sentence will stand without the phrase or clause between the commas.

"Often I have lain thus, when the fact would come over me with such overpowering force as to break the icy spell . . ."

What fact? It makes sense only if you already know what "the fact" is that broke the icy spell. Of course, this example has been contaminated, because we've read the full sentence and we know about the death grip. But if you came to the sentence fresh it would not make sense unless you knew which fact came over White-Jacket (he might freeze to death) to move him to action. If the clause is integral to the meaning of the sentence, it should not be set off by commas. It is restrictive, that intimidating word wielded by grammarians in the attempt to fend off commas. (People think we live to put commas in, but it isn't so.) A phrase is restrictive if it tightens the meaning, if it draws an invisible belt around which fact, out of all the facts in the universe, pertains.

So here is the sentence repunctuated (in part):

"Often I have lain thus, when the fact that if I laid much longer I would actually freeze to death would come over me with such overpowering force as to break the icy spell, and starting to my feet, I would endeavour to go through the combined manual and pedal exercise to restore the circulation."

I automatically treated the comma after "death" as one of a pair (with the one before "that") and took it out. Commas, like nuns, often travel in pairs. Perhaps Melville (or his copy editor) thought the sentence needed a comma after "death" so that one wouldn't read "death would come over me." But the comma after "death" separates the subject from the verb—a cardinal sin. It's as if Melville had flung commas like darts while riding a swell at sea, and they went wide of the mark. He didn't need a comma after "death." Melville's word order (syntax) ensures that the parts of the sentence that belong together stay together.

If he had to have two commas, the following might have been more acceptable:

"Often I have lain thus, when the fact that, if I laid much longer, I would actually freeze to death would come over me . . ."

Let's give it the test by taking out the "if" clause:

"Often I have lain thus, when the fact that I would actually freeze to death would come over me with such overpowering force as to break the icy spell . . ."

Something is missing. The "would" demands some setup, the condition—the "if"—under which White-Jacket would freeze to death: "if I laid much longer." So we don't need those commas. In fact, we reject those commas. But Melville apparently liked them. He must have had a comma shaker the size of a hogshead.

The second half of the sentence—"and starting to my feet, I would endeavour to go through the combined manual and pedal exercise to restore the circulation"—could have used a pair of commas to set off "starting to my feet." The rule in such a construction is to use either two commas or none. If the sentence began with the phrase "Starting to my feet," one comma would be perfect, but because it occurs in a compound sentence, following the conjunction "and," there should be a comma on either side of it. You would never write, "And, I would endeavor to go through the combined manual and pedal exercise . . ."

"Often I have lain thus, when the fact that if I laid much longer I would actually freeze to death would come over me with such overpowering force as to break the icy spell, and, starting to my feet, I would endeavour to go through the combined manual and pedal exercise to restore the circulation."

Not only are the commas around the participial phrase logical but they reinforce the meaning: the stop and start have the effect of sudden movement, ejecting White-Jacket from the sentence as from an ice-cube tray. You could do without the commas entirely:

"Often I have lain thus, when the fact that if I laid much longer I would actually freeze to death would come over me with such overpowering force as to break the icy spell, and starting to my feet I would endeavour to go through the combined manual and pedal exercise to restore the circulation."

But that would give you a postmodern Melville. The comma is a jolt upright. It gives the narrator time to struggle to his feet. And the uncluttered version seems to drain some of Melville's personality and leave a drier sentence, all juiced out. The commas add buoyancy.

Anyway, this rule that commas travel in pairs in introductory phrases following a conjunction is often broken. At *The New Yorker*, the official style is two commas or none, but many editors prefer the single comma and will break style when a sentence misreads. It's a compromise. I am half inclined to give Melville this one, as in this instance his nineteenth-century punctuation falls within modern guidelines, and punctuate the sentence thus:

"Often I have lain thus, when the fact that if I laid much longer I would actually freeze to death would come over me with such overpowering force as to break the icy spell, and starting to my feet, I would endeavour to go through the combined manual and pedal exercise to restore the circulation."

Melville has his tics, but he always puts his words in the right order. Once you fall under the spell of the writer, you look past those tics because you are more interested in what the writer says than in judging how well he grasped the editorial conventions of his time.

———

The New Yorker practices a "close" style of punctuation. We separate introductory clauses with a comma (though not necessarily in fiction), but not when they follow a conjunction (except "since" or "although") or when the meaning is restrictive. It's not always easy to decide what's restrictive. That's where judgment comes in. For instance, here is a sentence, chock-full of commas, that was quoted by Ben Yagoda in an online article for the *New York Times*: "Before Atwater died, of brain cancer, in 1991, he expressed regret . . ." Yagoda wrote, "No other publication would put a comma after 'died' or 'cancer.' *The New Yorker* does so because otherwise (or so the thinking goes), the sentence would suggest that Atwater died multiple times and of multiple causes." He added, "That is nutty, of course." The *Times*—and Yagoda, who teaches journalism—prefers an "open" style of punctuation, where all the words stream together and every phrase or clause is of equal moment, leaving the reader to figure it out. Some readers are especially proud of their ability to figure it out and like to write letters of complaint and, put, a, comma, after, every, word, to show us the error of our ways.

Secretly, I agreed with Yagoda. Once, when I was working on a Gould proof—transferring changes from Eleanor's proof onto a Reader's proof—I had the unsettling thought "What if Eleanor ever loses it?" What if all these commas and hyphens and subtleties of usage prove to be the products of a benign delusion? During the Reagan administration, everyone knew that Reagan had some form of dementia, but no one could do anything about it. The country was running on automatic. What if that was the case with Eleanor and *The New Yorker*? She was getting old, and she went deaf in her later years, so she was tragically isolated from the sounds of speech that were represented in the words she groomed. There was not a single thing anyone would be able to do about it. No one would enter the copy department and say to Eleanor, "Drop the pencil and step away from the desk." We were in her thrall, as the nation was in Reagan's thrall. I jumped up and went to my boss's office and said, "What if Eleanor goes crazy?" From the expression on her face—"You're only figuring this out now?"—I knew that we were all well advanced down the path.

Having been teased in the *Times* about *New Yorker* commas, I took a good hard look at the comma shaker, Lu Burke's protest against the indiscriminate sprinkling of commas. In fact these commas were not indiscriminate. They marked off segments of the sentence that were not germane to the meaning. The point of the sentence Yagoda had chosen for mild ridicule is that Atwater expressed regret before he died. What he died of and when he died of it are both extra details that the author, Jane Mayer, provides only to satisfy the reader's curiosity. Cause and date of death are not essential to the meaning of the sentence. They are nonrestrictive. I might even have been tempted to bury the obituary in parentheses, like a whisper: "Before Atwater died (of brain cancer, in 1991), he expressed regret . . ." Parentheses often act like giant commas, and commas like tiny parentheses. And it struck me as sad that anyone could be so distracted by the punctuation of a sentence that he failed to absorb the meaning of the words.

A while later, I received a letter objecting to the commas in this opening sentence of a piece by Marc Fisher: "When I was in high school, at Horace Mann, in the Bronx, in the nineteen-seventies, everyone took pride in the brilliant eccentricity of our teachers." The gist of that sentence is that at Horace Mann students enjoyed interacting with their crazy teachers. But if all you see when you read it is the commas, you miss that. Close punctuation is not meant as a guide to stops and starts, like Dickens's and Melville's commas. *The New Yorker* isn't asking you to pause and gasp for breath at every comma. That's not what close punctuation is about. The commas are marking a thoughtful subordination of information. I really don't see how any of them could be done without. The writer went to only one high school, a very special one-of-a-kind private school that happened to be in the Bronx, and the time that he went there was the nineteen-seventies. None of that is particularly interesting except in the context of a piece that promises to be about the bond between students and teachers. The punctuation is almost like Braille, providing a kind of bas-relief, accentuating the topography of the sentence. It looks choppy, but you don't have to chop it up when you read it. It is Aldo Manuzio's comma taken to its logical extreme. It's not insane—it's not even nutty. It's just showing what's important in the sentence in a subtle way. Another publication would let you figure it out for yourself. And, if that's what you want, you can always read some other magazine.

———

In the summer of 2013, in New Haven, where I had gone for the wedding of a friend, I picked up a copy of *Light Years*, by James Salter. I started it in an old hotel, the Duncan, feeling slightly sad that I had never gotten to go to Yale and wondering if I would have access to my friend, a delightful combination of a Catholic and a classicist, now that he was married. *Light Years* is about a marriage, its surface—an enviable round of dinner parties and indulgent Christmas projects (the daughters of the house actually have a pony) in a picture-postcard setting within commuting distance of Manhattan—and its coming apart from underneath. James Salter is a pen name. The writer's name was James Horowitz. His fiction had never run in *The New Yorker*, but the staff writer Nick Paumgarten had recently written a long piece about him, and there was so much buzz about it in the office that I read it on my own time.

This was my first taste of James Salter himself, and his prose is exquisite, so well groomed that I was surprised to come to a sentence with what I considered a superfluous comma: "Eve was across the room in a thin, burgundy dress that showed the faint outline of her stomach." It stopped me.

One of my duties as an apprentice on the copydesk was setting up the Christmas shopping lists that *The New Yorker* ran: columns and columns of merchandise, padded with as much charm as possible. There were gifts for children and for men, gifts for the house, and columns and columns about gourmet food, but it was the gifts for women that gave me the hardest time. Shopping for women invariably involved shopping for clothes, which meant strings of adjectives for color and fabric and nap and neckline and sleeve length: "old-fashioned Alpine house shoes, made of mouse-colored cattle-hair felt," "an Anna Karenina muff of purple suède with a lavish trim of red and black fox fur and with a hidden zippered pocket-purse" ($985!), "coats in dense and furlike hand-knitted angora," "roomy, below-the-knee culottes," "a floor-length cardigan coat in leaf-patterned black silk jacquard" (followed by the price, the store—sometimes a possessive—and the address, all punctuated with military precision). I would get lost in the throngs of adjectives. What are the rules governing a comma between adjectives preceding a noun? I studied the Gould proofs, trying to divine the difference between the qualities that an adjective conferred on a noun and why sometimes whole long strings of them did not call for any commas. The usage guides say that if you can substitute "and" for the comma it belongs there. I gave James Salter the "and" test, and "thin and burgundy" did not pass. If this had crossed my desk, I would have taken the comma out and made it "a thin burgundy dress."

The logic behind this rule is that the two adjectives are not coordinate: they do not belong to the same order. One adjective ("burgundy") clings more tenaciously to the noun ("dress") than the other ("thin"). Bryan Garner, the expert in American usage, offers another test: reverse the order of the adjectives. Would you ever say "a burgundy, thin dress"? I wouldn't.

I wondered whether this was the author's comma or whether it had slipped past the copy editor. I doubted that it was something a copy editor would add. This edition of *Light*

Years was typographically flawless. Was it possible that the comma was retained at the author's insistence? Consider the context: "Eve was across the room in a thin, burgundy dress that showed the faint outline of her stomach." Was the author trying to emphasize the thinness of the fabric in order to linger over the "faint outline" of her stomach? If so, I thought he was misguided, not to say lecherous. (Her name is Eve: she's obviously a temptress.) But was I going to let a superfluous comma prevent me from enjoying a good read? It didn't stop me in Dickens, and it wouldn't stop me in Salter. I persisted.

I have to admit that I was not completely impartial. *Light Years* had an introduction by Richard Ford, whose work I once tried to take a comma out of. The offending comma followed the word "So" at the beginning of a line of dialogue, and Ford preferred to retain it. The choice of Richard Ford for the introduction suggested to me that James Salter, like Richard Ford, might be stubborn about his punctuation. He might be one of the "ear" guys, the ones who think they have to orchestrate each sentence. I didn't read Ford's introduction. I never read an introduction that is not by the author: I find that it gets in the way, and can even prevent me from reading the book. I once tried to read *Ivanhoe*, because it was cited in some children's series—Trixie Belden or Betsy and Tacy—and I got so bogged down in the scholarly pages with lowercase roman numerals that I never got to Sir Walter Scott. I still have never read *Ivanhoe*.

Then it happened again: "She smiled that stunning, wide smile." The phrase "stunning and wide" doesn't make it for me, and neither does "wide and stunning" (although I would have read right over "wide, stunning smile"). The narrator has already remarked on the wideness of the character's smile (hence the "that" in "that stunning, wide smile") and is intensifying its attractiveness at the second reference. "Stunning" qualifies the wide smile. Adjectives not coordinate. No comma.

Again: "It was as if they were aboard ship: some old, island steamer." An "island steamer" is a kind of boat. There is no danger of someone's misreading the phrase as a steamer from "some old island."

And another nautical reference: "The ship was enormous . . . the vastness of its black, stained side overwhelmed them." This comma seems to be trying to repel a hyphen hovering between "black" and "stained." It is not a "black-stained side" but a black side, stained: a black stained side.

I'll say it again: It's not that these four extraneous (to my ear) commas diminished my enjoyment of the book, but I did stop and wonder where they came from, the author or the editor, and whether there was any discussion about them. James Salter clearly has a sharp ear and a fine eye. His pen name evokes the word "psalter" while suggesting earthiness. In doing without a hyphen in the title *Light Years* (*Webster's* spells it "light-year"), he cubes the meaning: carefree years, seen from an astronomical distance. Just for balance, here is one of his finest commas: "He sailed on the *France* in the noisy, sad afternoon." Sad and noisy, noisy and sad. "Noisy" is especially effective because it evokes "nausea," from the Greek for "seasickness." Could a writer so sensitive to language have a thing for kinky punctuation?

It was enough to make me doubt my comma sense. Some days, "thin and burgundy" sounded just fine. At work, coming to the phrase "a stout, middle-aged woman," I automatically started to pluck the comma out and then became unsure. "Stout and middle-aged"? I don't think so. "Middle-aged and stout"?

Definitely not. Wasn't it the same as "a fat old lady"? "Fat and old"? "Old and fat"? An old fat lady? "An old fat lady" suggests that the fat lady in the circus is being hounded out of her job by an ambitious new fat lady, at which point she will become just another fat old lady. I was driving myself mad.

I decided to write to James Salter and ask him about his commas. He wrote back:

"I sometimes ignore the rules about commas although generally I follow convention and adhere to the advice in Strunk and White. Punctuation is for clarity and also emphasis, but I also feel that, if the writing warrants it, punctuation can contribute to the music and rhythm of the sentences. You don't get permission for this, of course; you take the liberty."

When a writer who is not a poet invokes rhythm, copy editors often exchange looks . . . But James Salter went on to describe the reasoning behind each of the commas in question. As I had suspected, with the comma in "Eve was across the room in a thin, burgundy dress that showed the faint outline of her stomach," he was trying to emphasize the contours of the stomach under the dress. "It wasn't a thin burgundy dress," he wrote. "It was a thin dress, burgundy in color. I wanted the reader to be aware of the thinness. So you are right. The copy editor probably marked out the comma, and I wrote stet." He was doing the same thing with "stunning, wide smile," trying to control the impact of the "stunning" by smacking it with a comma as one would put English on a cue ball. Of my next example, he wrote, "I suppose that there's no chance of a reader thinking it's an old island, but I felt an instant of hesitation about old and island as I read the words and wanted to eliminate that." For this reader, the comma added rather than eliminated the hesitation. As for the last, he wrote,

"I think black stained side is too loose. It's not, as you say, black-stained, but black and also stained. The comma fixes that." His use of the word "loose" reinforces that metaphor for punctuation suggested by Melville: it tightens the prose, makes it shipshape. Though Manuzio invented the comma in order to separate parts of a sentence, it can tie words together as efficiently as it keeps them apart.

I suspect that Lu Burke would scoff at these explanations, but I am grateful for them, even if James Salter does have some untoward ideas about what you can do with commas and imputes to them a power that verges on magic. The writer is not always the best judge of his own effects, but at least he's thinking about it. The comma does not fix everything. Sometimes it gets in the way. He ended his letter with a recommendation for further reading: "The commas are better in *A Sport and a Pastime*."

———

My heart leaped up when I read in the *Times* about an appearance by three stellar British writers—Salman Rushdie introducing a conversation between Martin Amis and Ian McEwan. The reporter, Jennifer Schuessler, described them as "the Three Tenors" of the literary world. Audience members had submitted questions, which Rushdie read aloud. One of the questions was "Is there anything in your books that you wish you could change?" As Schuessler noted, it was poignant to hear Rushdie read the question aloud. McEwan "admitted he'd like to kill some commas in his first story collection." This was just the kind of confession that I had been secretly hoping to elicit from James Salter. But it turned out that McEwan meant not superfluous commas that he had stubbornly insisted on but commas pressed into service in place of periods, in defiance of grammar-school teachers everywhere, who call this a "comma fault": the separation of full sentences by a comma instead of a period. It's all right in something like "I came, I saw, I conquered," but in anything longer the period is not just preferred but dictated. It's an inarguable tenet of punctuation: the period at the end of the sentence makes you stop and tells you that a new sentence is about to begin. Otherwise you have the despicable "run-on sentence." And yet sometimes in fiction of a very high order you see sentences that have been spliced together with commas and you wonder . . . Chances are that if the piece has been published, the commas are not a mistake: someone, probably the author, insisted. The express-style sentences may be telling you something about the narrator. The Italian writer Elena Ferrante (a pen name) rushes from one sentence to the next, with a breathless pause, and the cumulative effect is of great urgency in the storytelling. I wasn't able to find McEwan's early collection; perhaps on account of those commas it has been suppressed. Anyway, he seems to have repented. I've copy-edited excerpts from his novels that ran in *The New Yorker*, and I don't remember encountering any noxious commas in the terminal position. "I fell under Beckett's spell," McEwan said of his early efforts. "I thought it was jolly cunning to have commas and not full stops. But now it doesn't look cunning at all."

Now, there's a writer who would have fewer regrets if he had listened to his copy editor.

Chapter 6

WHO PUT THE HYPHEN
IN *MOBY-DICK*?

I ALWAYS WANTED TO WRITE A BOOK, but it looked really hard: how did you get all the lines to come out even on the right-hand side of the page? I puzzled over this with a toy typewriter in the basement as a girl, never dreaming that one day all I would have to do is click on the icon for "justify right," and the words would automatically swell or squeeze to fit a line. Justification was never the writer's problem, anyway, but the typesetter's, and ever since Gutenberg the typesetter has had a friend in the hyphen, always at hand to break a word, with or without regard for pronunciation or etymology.

People have surprisingly strong feelings about word breaks. A long time ago I met a man on a ship in the Dodecanese who complained to me about the way *The New Yorker* broke "English" and "England." We follow *Merriam-Webster's*, which divides words phonetically, giving us "En-glish," "En-gland." *Webster's*

New World Dictionary (among others) divides words along meaningful units and goes with "Eng-lish" and "Eng-land." What bothered my shipmate was the way "glish" and "gland" looked on the next line, especially at the top of a column.

What bothered me was that here in the Aegean an American—a college English professor, to judge by the tan Hush Puppies he wore—was grilling me about word breaks. (He also complained about his subscription.) The truth is that I, too, disliked it: "glish" and "gland" are unsightly stand-alones. Yet I was deeply invested in our way of doing it and resentful about having to defend it while I was on vacation.

Those were the days of hot lead and picas. A typesetter would actually have to move the *g* manually down to the next line to achieve this unpopular effect. When we moved to cold type, in the early eighties, at first the computer didn't know how to break words. "Bedroom" would be hyphenated "be-droom." Somebody has since fed the computer an entire dictionary, complete with word breaks, and given copy editors the ability to hyphenate words by themselves. I simply put my cursor between the *n* and the *g* and hit option-shift-hyphen, and have my way with "En-glish." But the language is propagating faster than technology can keep up with it. In the *New York Times*, I have seen "ret-weet" (retweet) and "ju-ghandle" (jughandle, as in New Jersey's famous left-hand turns from the right-hand lane) and "Toscaes-que" (Toscaesque; that will teach you to make operatic references). As long as print is justified, there will be a place for humans in this business.

Because English has so many words of foreign origin, and words that look the same but mean something different depending on their context, and words that are in flux, opening and closing like flowers in time-lapse photography, the human element is especially important if we are to stay on top of the computers, which, in their determination to do our job for us, make decisions so subversive that even professional wordsmiths are taken by surprise. Once, in a piece that was about to go to press, I noticed that the word "cashier" was broken "ca-shier." Curious because "cash-ier" seemed obvious, I looked it up and found that *Webster's* has two distinct entries: "ca-shier," a transitive verb, meaning "to dismiss from service," especially "to dismiss dishonorably," with the synonyms "reject, discard"; and "cash-ier," a noun, meaning "one that has charge of money." (My first ambition was to be a cashier—I thought you got to keep all the money.) The computer, not knowing the difference between "cashier" the verb and "cashier" the noun, had chosen the first option.

It happened again with the word "bumper": it was broken "bum-per." Who doesn't know that the word "bumper" breaks after the "bump"? Back to the dictionary: The first entry for "bumper" is indeed "bum-per," a noun that means "a brimming cup or glass." I'll have a bumper of your finest IPA, my good man. The second sense, also divided "bum-per," is an adjective meaning "unusually large," as in "bumper crop." Finally, the third sense is rendered "bump-er," a noun, meaning "one that bumps" or "a device for absorbing shock or preventing damage (as in collision); *specif.* a bar at either end of an automobile." Ah! So the computer, regurgitating the dictionary, did not make it down to the form of the word in which *er* is a suffix. I moved my cursor between the *p* and the *e* and hit option-shift-hyphen. I am ever on the alert for bumpers and cashiers.

The hyphen leads a double life: it is used not just to break words into syllables but to tie two or more words together, in the formation of compounds. Here are three compounds: school bus, bus driver, school-bus driver. This is one of the simpler uses of the hyphen, turning compound nouns into adjectives. You could also have "bus-driver hero." "Ice cream" is two words as a noun and hyphenated as an adjective in "ice-cream cone" or "ice-cream sandwich." You can get carried away with hyphens: putting them in, taking them out, putting them back in again. When I took a copy-editing test, I agonized over whether or not to put a hyphen in the phrase "bright red car." Did "bright" modify the shade of red or the car? I put it in, I took it out, put it in, took it out. Only when I had taken the hyphen out and turned the test in did it become clear to me that I should have put the hyphen in. The car was bright red. It was a bright-red car.

There is a phase in the life of every copy editor when she is obsessed with hyphens. The laughing hyphena. When I was learning my way around on the copydesk, I noted the two schools of hyphenation: Eleanor Gould seemed to hyphenate everything, and Lu Burke hated anything extra. Lu taught me to do without hyphens when a word is in quotation marks, unless the word is always hyphenated; the quotation marks alone hold the words together, and it would be overkill to link them with a hyphen as well. (Capital letters and italics work the same way.) Eleanor once mystified me by putting a hyphen in "blue stained glass" to make it "blue-stained glass." When I asked her about it, she took on an oracular look, and allowed that it was a difficult concept. I had the impression that I would never grasp it. Is it stained glass that is blue? Or glass that is blue-stained? The answer would seem to be: both. If commas are open to interpretation, hyphens are downright Delphic.

Eleanor was also a judicious withholder of hyphens. It was her judgment that a "nuclear power plant" did not call for a hyphen, because it was both a power plant that happened to be nuclear *and* a plant that supplied nuclear power. There are other compounds that are not quite as double-jointed as nuclear power plants, but that still tempt people to put unnecessary hyphens in them. For example, "high blood pressure." You can take it apart into "high" and "blood pressure"—that is, one can suffer from blood pressure that is high—but you cannot yoke together "high blood" and expect it to modify "pressure." Someone might be tempted to hyphenate "adult cable television," but what is an adult cable? You might refer to cable TV for adults as "adult cable," but it's not the same thing. A harrowing example is "baby back ribs." They are not the ribs of a baby back but the back ribs of, yes, a baby. If you must order baby back ribs, try thinking of "baby" as meaning "miniature" instead of "wee creature." Or become a vegetarian.

A phrase that teeters on the edge is "bad hair day." Is a bad hair day like a Lu Burke day? That is what I say at the office when I am feeling especially irritable: that I am having a Lu Burke day. Lu had her virtues, but she could be bad-tempered. When she was angry or frustrated, for whatever reason, she would descend like a tornado on anyone who had the bad luck to be in her path. She reminded one of my colleagues of that cartoon Tasmanian Devil—a spinning, whirling ball of fury that would bite anyone or anything that got in its way. It helped to see this as comic: you could not take the behavior of a Tasmanian Devil personally, and

Lu's tirades were essentially harmless. According to Lu's own logic, there would be a hyphen in "bad-hair day." I like it better without the hyphen, though I don't know that the compound "hair day" has any meaning. How was your hair day, dear? Have a fabulous hair day! The more you say it, the better it sounds. If Eleanor could hyphenate "blue-stained glass," and Lu could throw a tantrum in the hall, I think I can hold the hyphen out of "bad hair day."

Lu Burke once ridiculed a new copy editor who had come from another publication for taking the hyphen out of "pan-fry." "But it's in Web," the novice chirped. "What are you even looking in the dictionary for?" Lu said, and I wish there were a way of styling that sentence so that you could see it getting louder and more incredulous toward the end. She spoke it in a crescendo, like Ralph Kramden, on *The Honeymooners*, saying, "Because I've got a BIG *MOUTH!*" Without the hyphen, "panfry" looks like "pantry." "Panfree!" Lu guffawed, and said it again. "Panfree!" The copy editor was just following the rules, but Lu said she had no "word sense." Lu was especially scornful of unnecessary hyphens in adverbs like "feet first" and "head on." Of course, "head on" is hyphenated as an adjective in front of a noun—"The editors met in a head-on collision"—but in context there is no way of misreading "The editors clashed head on in the hall." The novice argued that "head on" was ambiguous without the hyphen. Lu was incredulous. "Head on what?" she howled, over and over, as if it were an uproarious punch line. Eventually, that copy editor went back to where she had come from. "It's as if I tried to become a nun and failed," she confided. It did sometimes feel as if we belonged to some strange cloistered order, the Sisters of the Holy Humility of Hyphens.

The writer-editor Veronica Geng once physically restrained me from looking in the dictionary for the word "hairpiece," because she was afraid that the dictionary would make it two words and that I would follow it blindly. As soon as she left the office, I did look it up, and it was two words, but I respected her word sense and left it alone. I once made "hairstyle" one word, having found it in *Webster's*, and Lu appeared in my doorway instantaneously, like a fire engine screaming around the corner two seconds after you've pulled a false alarm. "We don't close up 'style' compounds," she said instructively. (She was having a good hair day.) I knew we made "life style" two words, but I thought it was because we disapproved of the concept of a "lifestyle," and that was our way of showing it. I was learning that the dictionary is a wonderful thing, but you can't let it push you around, especially where compound words are concerned. Also that a hyphen is not a moral issue.

The received wisdom about compounds is that they start out as two words, acquire a transitional hyphen, and then lose the hyphen, becoming one word. "Today" used to be hyphenated. "Ringtone" was two words for about a nanosecond before solidifying, skipping the hyphen stage completely. "Deluxe," which started out as two French words (*de luxe*), was hyphenated at *The New Yorker* until February 5, 2003, when an editor in a particularly foul mood threw a fit and ripped the hyphen out of it. While I have to admit that "de-luxe" was quaint, the old-fashioned form seemed more luxurious to me, upholstered like a divan. Removing the hyphen made it into something you'd find on the menu at the local diner: Cheeseburger Deluxe.

The awful truth about hyphens and copy editors is that if there is one you want to take it out and if there's not one you're tempted to put one in. If we had to cast each hyphen individually, like Gutenberg's punch cutter, we would be more sparing in our use of them. At least we'd have time to think about it. I like the hyphen in "high-school principal" because there actually is such a word as "school principal," and if the school principal is high she should be escorted off the premises and given a TV series. A "high-school student" is perhaps fussier than necessary (who refers to "a school student"?), but, as with the serial comma, it's easier to make up your mind and be consistent than it is to mull over every instance. And what's wrong with being fussy? That's what we're getting paid for. Then again, what's wrong with mulling over every instance?

In a story by Karen Russell, a boy is making fun of a girl who went to church, and asks, "How was it? . . . Delicious God-bread?" I was persuaded by another proofreader—another unique person with her own ideas and the brief to impose them—to remove the hyphen in "God-bread" and make it two words. But it bothered me without the hyphen, and later, walking back to the office after brooding over a sandwich, I realized that the analogy was not with, say, "raisin bread": "God bread" was not studded with gods. It *was* God. First chance I got, I restored the hyphen in "God-bread." Transubstantiation in a hyphen.

The best thing ever written about hyphens is *Meet Mr. Hyphen (And Put Him in His Place)*, by Edward N. Teall, published by Funk & Wagnalls in 1937. For one thing, it may be the only full-length work on hyphens extant in English. Although written for the profession, for makers of style guides, it is entertaining enough for a general reader. Considering the rate at which the language changes, it's incredible that a study of hyphens from three generations ago remains relevant. Mr. Hyphen was onto something. Teall, who lived from 1880 to 1947, and who was a graduate of Princeton (class of 1902), was descended from people who cared passionately about language. "My father specialized in the field of the compound word," he writes. "We of his household may be said to have lived on hyphens. We did this figuratively, in that we heard them much discussed; literally, in that they translated into food, shelter, clothing and recreation, since they furnished the head of the house with remunerative employment." Teall was preternaturally gifted—he knew what would bother us in the future. He considers the "amazing present-day high school fad *alright*" (though he does not really like to think of "all right" as a compound; notice he does without a hyphen in "high school") and was decades ahead of *The Honeymooners* in his learned footnote on "po-lop-o-ny," a nonexistent word modeled on "polyphony" and created when you close up "polo pony." He also makes frequent references to compounds that occupy a "twilight zone." Compounding is not a science, he says. "It should be regarded as an art, because personal preferences and individual judgments will always be decisive." He says, "Good compounding is a manifestation of character."

The word "hyphen" is from the Greek (which I should have known, from the *hy* and the *ph* in its spelling) and was originally an adverb meaning "together." In form it was a curved horizontal line, set below the baseline: an open parenthesis lying on its back. It functions like the tie in music notation. Teall has a familiarity with the subject that comes from a lifetime of study and experimentation. He uses "hyphen" as noun and verb (rather than "hyphenate"), and speaks of ancient compounds that have "coalesced" into one word ("husband" is from the Anglo-Saxon *hus* and *bonda*, meaning "head of the house") and of "one-wording" a compound.

"Nothing is to be gained by making a sacred cow out of compounding—nor yet by dismissing it as a hobby of the language cranks," he writes. "It is puzzling, difficult—but not an unfathomable mystery, not impossible of practical treatment. Neither those who sidestep it nor those who turn it into a nightmare are doing right." In capitals, he writes, "THE PRIME NECESSITY IS TO SAFEGUARD AGAINST MISREADING." The hyphen is like the comma in this: follow some rules, sure, but in the end what you're after is clarity of meaning.

One bad habit Teall wishes to cure us of right away is mistreating the hyphen by putting it between an adverb ending in *ly* and a participle. His example is a headline: "Use of 'Methodist' Is Newly-Defined." Lavishing sympathy on the hyphen, he laments, "Did you ever see a hyphen more completely wasted? A hyphen more unnecessarily and fruitlessly employed?" Even in such a frequently used compound as "well known," Teall would omit the hyphen in both the attributive and the predicate position. (*The New Yorker* follows him halfway, omitting the hyphen in the predicate position—"The man is well read"—but employing it in the attributive: "I like a well-read man." However, if you further qualify it by saying "I like a very well read man," the hyphen wants to pop back out again. The damn thing really does have a life of its own.)

The easiest compounds to codify are adjectives formed from the past participle (irregular or formed with -*ed*) preceded by an adjective, a noun, or an adverb that does not end in *ly*. Teall's list includes such classics as hard-boiled (*The New Yorker* uses the hyphen for the egg and one-words it for a person), long-winded, soft-hearted, tight-fisted, and hyphen-minded. All these compounds take the hyphen. Of these, only "soft-hearted" has lost its hyphen. Teall also admits to this club the combinations with the adverb "well" (well read, well told), which he prefers as two words, but he is so delighted that one rule covers so many compounds that he suppresses his personal preference. Still, he draws the line—again—at using a hyphen in phrases such as "a badly-torn book." These are "monstrosities" representing "an excess of academic affectation."

Each compound needs to have its parts analyzed before you can place or withhold the hyphen or make it into one word or two. Participles (the *-ing* form of the verb) sometimes function more like nouns than like adjectives, even if they look like adjectives. A "laughing stock" is not a stock that laughs, and a "walking stick" is not a stick that walks (unless we're talking about an insect). Teall says that these participles form a function of "identification." Examples are numerous: "working clothes" (the clothes don't work; they are donned for working), "ironing board" (the board doesn't iron; it is used for ironing), "whirling dervish" (yes, it is a dervish that whirls, but not "casually," as he says; rather, the whirling dervish "is a member of a cult whose practice whirling is ritual," making it distinct "from other kinds of dervishes"; "whirling" identifies the dervish). In his own words, Teall is making the same distinction that we mean by "restrictive."

Teall feels that the words that lose the hyphen and become solid tend to be figurative (cowcatcher), while the ones that retain the hyphen are literal (bronco-buster). The same logic seems to be behind *The New Yorker*'s decision about "hard-boiled" and "hardboiled." I absorbed a version of this on the copydesk. A dog-lover is one who loves dogs; the dogs are the object of his love. James Thurber was a dog-lover. A dog lover, without the hyphen, is still a dog—the Tramp, say, in *Lady and the Tramp*. (Grammar via Disney!) A bird-watcher is a watcher of birds; a bird watcher would be a bird that keeps an eye on things. You can actually hear the difference (and feel the bird's eye on you).

This was brought home to me when a woman from California, one Alice Russell-Shapiro, wrote a letter to the editor—the copy editor—of *The New Yorker* complaining about (among other things) the term "star fucker." She was not the least offended by seeing the term in print, only by its lack of what she called the "activating hyphen." I wonder whether she was a distant relative of Edward Teall's—certainly they are both gifted explicators of the hyphen. In "star fucker," without the hyphen, each word has equal weight: a fucker who is a star. But in "star-fucker" the hyphen tips the weight to the first element, the object (star) of the activity embodied in the noun (fucking).

There is one other way to keep the "cow" out of "co-workers": where two vowels rub up against each other, a diaeresis may be used instead of a hyphen. Often mistakenly called an umlaut, a diaeresis (pronounced "die heiresses"; it's from the Greek for "divide," and is devilishly hard to spell) consists of two dots carefully centered over the second vowel in such words as "naïve" and "reëlection." An umlaut is a German thing that alters the pronunciation of a vowel (Brünnhilde) and often changes the meaning of a word: *schon* (adv.), already; *schön* (adj.), beautiful. In German, if an umlaut appears in a combination of two vowels, it will go over the first vowel, and it indicates something important: a plural, say. A diaeresis always goes over the second vowel, and it means that the vowel is leading off a separate syllable.

Most of the English-speaking world finds the diaeresis inessential. *The New Yorker* may be the only publication in America that uses it regularly. It's actually a lot of trouble, these days, to get the diaeresis to stick over the vowel. The autocorrect whisks it off, and you have to go back, highlight the letter, hold down the option key while pressing the *u*, and then retype the appropriate letter. The question is: Why bother? Especially since the diaeresis is the single thing that readers of the letter-writing variety complain about most.

Basically, we have three options for these kinds of words: "cooperate," "co-operate," and "coöperate." Back when the magazine was just developing its style, someone decided that the first could be misread and the second was ridiculous, and so adopted the third as the most elegant solution with the broadest application. By the thirties, when Mr. Hyphen was considering these things, the diaeresis was already almost obsolete, and he was through with it. He was for letting people figure things out for themselves. The fact is that, absent the two dots, most people would not trip over the "coop" in "cooperate" or the "reel" in "reelect," though they might pronounce the "zoo" in "zoological" (and we don't use the diaeresis for that).

Not everyone at *The New Yorker* is devoted to the diaeresis. Some have wondered why it's still hanging around. Style does change sometimes. For instance, back in the eighties, the editors decided to modernize by moving the semicolon outside of the closing quotation mark. A notice went up on the bulletin board that began, "Adjust your reflexes."

Lu Burke used to pester the style editor, Hobie Weekes, who had been at the magazine since 1928, to get rid of the diaeresis. Like Mr. Hyphen, Lu was a modern independent-minded reader, and she didn't need to have her vowels micromanaged. Once, in the elevator, Weekes seemed to be weakening. He told her he was on the verge of changing that style and would be sending out a memo soon. And then he died.

This was in 1978. No one has had the nerve to raise the subject since.

———

The holiest hyphen in literature is the hyphen in *Moby-Dick*. Whenever the book was mentioned in print, I wondered: Why is the title hyphenated when the whale himself did not use the hyphen? Can Herman Melville, that demon punctuator, have insisted on it? Who put the hyphen in *Moby-Dick*?

I am not a Melville scholar, but ever since I read *Moby-Dick* Melville has been following me around. I graduated from college as an English major without having read anything by Melville, so the year between college and graduate school, when I'd moved back to Cleveland and was living with my parents and working in the costume company, I tackled it. I latched on to the motto "Oh, Time, Strength, Cash, and Patience!" It comes at the end of Chapter 32, "Cetology," on the taxonomy of the whale. It is well worth the "ponderous task" of pressing on from the Grampus through the Trumpa, the Fin-Back, the Humpbacked, the Nar- whale and the Killer to the Huzza Porpoise and the Quog. The motto served me well through graduate school. Back in Cleve- land was a poster of scenes from *Moby-Dick* that my father had framed for me, and years later I brought it out to Rockaway and hung it in what came to be called the Moby Dick room. During the surge of Hurricane Sandy in 2012, the ocean came to within a centimeter of the frame.

I read the book a second time on a trip to Nantucket, and dipped into it again when I was invited to participate in a project organized by Philip Hoare, the author of *The Whale*: a chapter a day, every chapter read by a different person, posted online with art work. Each voice and the enthusiasm of each reader for the assigned chapter kept the story fresh. I read Chapter 6, "The Street," about New Bedford, whence Ishmael embarks for Nantucket to sign onto the *Pequod*. Philip Hoare had visited all the sights associated with Melville and his research into the leviathan, sniffing ambergris in one museum, catching the scent of oil that lingered in the reconstructed skeleton of a whale in another, whale-watching off Provincetown. So I decided to follow in his footsteps, stopping in New Bedford to smell the roses on my way to the Cape ("And the women of New Bedford, they bloom like their own red roses"). Hoare also re-creates a picnic on Mount Greylock, in the Berkshires—the moment when Melville met Hawthorne. On a trip to the Berkshires undertaken for purely hedonistic reasons, I made a detour to Arrowhead, the house in Pittsfield where Melville wrote *Moby-Dick*. Though I did not expect Arrowhead to furnish an immediate answer to my question about that immortal hyphen, stuck like a harpoon in Melville's famous title, it seemed like as good a place as any to begin my research.

Arrowhead is a big yellow house at 780 Holmes Road, south of Pittsfield, with a blue sign outside in the shape of a sperm whale. A snowy, unplowed driveway led to a muddy parking lot with a view of Mount Greylock. Beyond several Berkshires-style outbuildings—a barn, a shed—I came to a door that opened as if by itself. "Are you here for the exhibition?" a wiry gray-haired woman asked. I looked around. There was a desk with shelves behind it featuring various editions of *Moby-Dick* and mugs and whale-shaped merchandise and a "Call Me Ishmael" T-shirt on a hanger.

"Isn't this where Melville's study is?" I asked.

"Yes, but today we have an exhibit of costumes," the woman said. "It's the only reason we're open." A boy with thick brown hair jumped up from the ticket desk and said, "It's closed, but I can take you up there. Since you came especially for that." He led me through some period rooms with mannequins in velvet dresses to a staircase with a "Closed" sign strung between the railings. The boy, whose name was Will, removed the sign and took me up the stairs. Suddenly I was in Melville's study.

"It's not his desk," Will said. The desk is in downtown Pittsfield, in the Athenaeum, a gorgeous historic building that I had passed on the way. "But it is his chair." The chair, elaborately carved, was positioned at a table so that its occupant commanded a view of Mount Greylock (named for an Indian chief). A pair of eyeglasses were placed on a manuscript letter on top of the table. "Those are his spectacles," Will said. "And many of these are his books." He gestured to a glass-fronted bookcase. "We have his large-print Shakespeare that someone sent him because his eyesight was bad." Melville had read Shakespeare and the Bible before revising *Moby-Dick*. "We call this the Hawthorne Room." Will indicated a spartan bedroom off the study with a narrow bed covered with a counterpane. Hawthorne visited Melville at

Arrowhead at least once, and it was after meeting Hawthorne, on Mount Greylock, and reading Shakespeare and the Bible, that Melville took his whaling saga to a deeper level.

A vitrine displayed a few Melville relics: a scrimshaw letter opener with a walrus carved on it, a change purse, a corkscrew. There was a harpoon, but it wasn't Melville's, Will admitted: "It's the right period, but it's just here for atmosphere." Leaning against the fireplace was a harpoon-shaped poker that *had* belonged to Melville.

I asked my guide if I might sit in Melville's chair. He shook his head. "You can touch it," he said. "It's fragile. It was in an attic." Did that mean it had the original upholstery? Was this the chair that Melville had sat his ass in to write? Will got called downstairs. He trusted me not to sit in the chair, so I stood behind it and looked over Melville's shoulders at the sun falling on a birch tree outside the wavy-glass window and the snow-covered fields stretching all the way to Mount Greylock. Melville had written of his view that it made him feel as if he were at sea and Greylock were a sperm whale.

Melville was born in New York City. His early books, *Typee* and *Omoo*, had been successful, all about native girls and cannibals—he was a kind of literary Gauguin. It was on the strength of those books that he had moved to the Berkshires to write. But *Moby-Dick* was a failure. Melville had a wife and children to support, and he was in debt to his in-laws, so he swapped his property in Pittsfield for a house on East Twenty-sixth Street in Manhattan that one of his in-laws had a mortgage on. He kept writing—*Pierre* was his next book—but he also took a job at the customs office and commuted downtown for the next twenty years. He never had another literary success. *Billy Budd* was published posthumously. His widow kept the manuscript in her breadbox.

Downstairs, I stocked up on souvenirs of Arrowhead. I had just lent a friend my Viking-Penguin edition of *Moby-Dick*, with its scholarly apparatus, and so I bought the Modern Library edition, from 1930, with woodcuts by Rockwell Kent, and no ponderous foreword or footnotes (except those written by Melville himself) or glossary of ship's parts—nothing to get between me and the text. The editors even resisted the hyphen in "Moby Dick." I also bought a ruler that says on it "Herman Melville's ARROWHEAD" and has a reproduction of a twenty-cent postage stamp with Melville's portrait and a quotation: "It is better to fail in originality, than to succeed in imitation" (Melville's comma).

I drove home, thinking of Melville and how, in 1863, he had moved back to New York in a spirit of defeat. Often I have sat in my car in front of a plaque marking the site of Melville's house, waiting for the street sweeper between seven-thirty and eight on Tuesday and Friday mornings, observing alternate-side-parking rules, and watching as aged beef and fresh linens were delivered to the freight entrance of the boutique hotel across the street. Melville's block is alternate-side-parking gold. There used to be a Staples where his house stood, which wasn't entirely inappropriate, but it moved a few blocks south and downsized, and the space is now occupied by a Spanish brasserie and a bank branch.

In the car, while trying to redeem time spent claiming a parking spot, I continued my pursuit of the hyphen in the white whale. There are a few huge biographies of Melville, and I chose one by Andrew Delbanco—*Melville: His World and Work*—to get a sense of Melville's life in publishing. There is no manuscript extant of *Moby-Dick*. Delbanco writes that Melville, so protective of his text, personally delivered the manuscript to the printer, on Fulton Street, and did his own proofreading. This was in August of 1851. Meanwhile, his brother Allan was negotiating on his behalf with a publisher in London. Allan Melville sent the London firm of Bentley a letter explaining that his brother had added a dedication (to Nathaniel Hawthorne) and changed the title from *The Whale* to *Moby-Dick*, who was, after all, the hero. The name Moby Dick was inspired by a real-life white whale known as Mocha Dick, who makes a cameo appearance in *White-Jacket*. The brother added, in an early, unsuccessful stab at marketing, "It is thought here that the new title will be a better *selling* title—." In his note, Allan Melville used the hyphen.

It was too late to change the title of the British edition. In September of 1851, two months before the American edition came out, the novel appeared in England under the title *The Whale*. The English publisher made many changes in the text, most of them traceable to prudery, religious scruple, or nationalism, and left off the end, with Ishmael afloat, in italics, on Queequeg's coffin. Somewhere along the line, Herman Melville gave up. Delbanco quotes from *Pierre* to describe the author's probable attitude while proofreading *Moby-Dick*: "The proofs . . . were replete with errors, but . . . he became impatient of such minute, gnat-like torments; he randomly corrected the worst, and let the rest go; jeering with himself at the rich harvest thus furnished to the entomological critics."

The biography led this entomological critic to remarks by G. Thomas Tanselle on nineteenth-century punctuation conventions: "Commas were sometimes used expressively to suggest the movements of voice, and capitals were sometimes meant to give significances to a word beyond those it might have in its uncapitalized form." Multiple editions of *Moby-Dick* later, the Library of America edition, using the Northwestern-Newberry edition, yielded up the information I was looking for, in a note by Tanselle buried on page 1428:

> In his letter Allan spells "Moby-Dick" with the hyphen, as it also appears on the title page and divisional title page of the American edition; but only one of the many occurrences of the name in the text includes the hyphen. The Northwestern-Newberry editors retain the hyphen in the title, arguing that hyphenated titles were conventional in mid-nineteenth-century America. As a result, the hyphenated form refers to the book, the unhyphenated to the whale.

> It was a copy editor who put the hyphen in *Moby-Dick*.

Chapter 7

A DASH, A SEMICOLON, AND A COLON WALK INTO A BAR

PUNCTUATION IS A DEEPLY CONSERVATIVE club. It hardly ever admits a new member. In the sixties, an adman invented the interrobang, a combined question mark and exclamation point, but it did not catch on. Still, considering that we have only a handful of tools—think of them as needles and pins in a sewing kit, or drill bits and screws in a tool chest—the variety of tics that writers develop and effects that they create is astonishing. Even the period, which marks the end of a conventional declarative sentence, can be nuanced, in context. I paged through Céline's *Death on the Installment Plan*, which Ed Stringham gave me decades ago and which I still have not found the right moment to read (it just does not sound like a beach book—less so the older I get), and saw sentences strung together like beads . . . Ellipses flowed on for page after page . . . It seemed very modern, like the tendency for an e-mail to trail off, inviting an answer . . . You realize after a while that when you come to the end nothing is going to seem as desperate as that final period.

Which piece of punctuation has the most gumption? You might think it is the exclamation point, also known as the screamer, because it is used sparingly and packs a punch. In German, every command ends with an exclamation point. One imagines that Germans bark at each other a lot. The question mark, by contrast, is gentle, a lazy Irishman. When an utterance is both interrogative and exclamatory—say, "What the devil"—people are sometimes tempted to use both a question mark and an exclamation point, but this is a bad idea. Word order will take care of the interrogative, while the bold exclamation point trumps the hesitant question mark every time.

The interior punctuation that goes on in sentences is even more subtle. It's like a family—we have built on the comma and the period, and come up with some pretty tough characters, as well as with some snobs and some sainted family members who are ready for anything. For instance, the dash family.

In case the conversation at the dinner table ever turns to dashes, it is best to be prepared. It can happen! You can hold the table spellbound with anecdotes about the dash family. For instance, when I was nine, we moved from a two-family house on West Thirty-ninth Street, on the West Side of Cleveland, out to Meadowbrook Avenue, which was all but technically in the suburbs. I was eager to move—I would have my own bedroom in a two-story house with a real fake fireplace—but I didn't realize until we were in the new house how much character the old neighborhood had had. It was on the edge of the zoo, and full of hillbillies and immigrants (DPs, in my mother's term: displaced persons), with last names like Munchauer, Sindelar, Kerfonta, and Sliwka (pronounced "slifka"; years later I learned that it was Polish for "plum"). The new neighborhood was on the other side of the zoo. There were no fences between the houses, and at first we interpreted that to mean that we could run through people's yards (strike one) and sit on people's benches (strike two) and coast down the driveway on our ancient oversized tricycle and up the driveway across the street (strike three). Our new neighbors had names like Blank and Dash. Mr. and Mrs. Blank were a crabby old couple who yelled at us when our badminton birdie landed on their lawn. We used a pair of my mother's clothes poles to retrieve it. The Dashes employed a diaper service and were customers of Charles' Chips, the house-to-house potato-chip vendor.

If you have no personal anecdotes to share about the Dashes, feel free to appropriate mine. But lowercase dashes also provide hours of dinner conversation. Dashes, like table forks, come in different sizes, and there is a proper use for each. The handiest member of the dash family is the one-em dash. Think of it as the dinner fork, the one on the inside, which you use for your main dish. The em is a printer's unit approximately the width of a capital letter *M*. We who grew up using typewriters learned to type two hyphens, with or without space on either side, to form a dash. Most word-processing programs automatically fuse double hyphens into a solid dash when you get to the end of the word following it—that is, the computer automatically compensates for old-fashioned habits. There is also a one-en dash, the width of a capital *N*. That would be your salad fork. Some clever writers type two one-ens instead of two hyphens to form the long dash, and it looks good, but it's brittle: if it falls on a line break, it snaps in half.

The en dash works more like a hyphen than like a dash, connecting compound words, such as the New York–New Haven Railroad. Many publications use the en dash when just one of the items is compound, like Minneapolis–St. Paul instead of Minneapolis-St. Paul (Minneapolitans might prefer that St. Paul not be mentioned at all), and some use it to relieve hyphen congestion, in a phrase such as "chocolate-chocolate-chip–ice-cream cone." I find this awkward, as if one leg were longer than the other. *The Chicago Manual of Style* considered doing away with the one-en dash, but has let it linger. It's useful in scores (22–1) and dates (1978–89), though it is not strictly necessary in either. A simple hyphen would do.

A sentence with its hyphens and its dashes of the proper length in their proper places is a great relief.

Before:

At the bar, flavor infused vodka –called aquavit – is another high point of the dining experience.

After:

At the bar, flavor-infused vodka—called aquavit—is another high point of the dining experience.

Think of all the uses of the dash:

—It can stand at the head of a line to indicate an item in a list.

—It can be deployed like a colon—it introduces an amplification of what has come before.

—It can be employed in pairs within a sentence—like the comma—and is subject to some of the same rules as the comma.

—It can be used instead of quotation marks to set off dialogue.

　　—Who does he think he is, James Joyce?

　　—He thinks quotation marks look fussy.

　　—OK, as long as the reader can tell who is speaking.

—It can create a sense of drama—false drama.

—It can be used within dialogue in place of a semicolon, and it is actually more realistic—most people don't think in semicolons.

—It can work as a defiant alternative to a period at the end—

—It can end a sentence abruptly to show that a thought has been inter—

—rupted. It can pick up where you left off.

With the switch to cold type, in the mid-1980s, copy editors were frustrated by the inability of the computer to recognize the dash as a legitimate piece of punctuation that needed to be connected to the word before it—the dash was routinely bumped down to the next line. Maybe this is a hangover of the preference, in some parts, for inserting a space on either side of the double hyphen: the spaced dash. We copy editors struggled like Atlas to hold each dash up there at the end of the line where it belonged. You would never kick a comma or a semicolon or a colon or a period down to the next line. (Well, unless the period in a dot-com falls at the end of a line and looks like the end of a sentence. The *New York Times* made the interesting decision to move that dot down to the beginning of the next line.) The *Times* freely sets dashes at the beginning of a line. Readers are used to it. I myself got tired of lobbying the makeup department to squeeze in the dash—I knew they all thought I was the world's biggest fussbudget. Now that word-processing programs have made us a nation of desktop publishers, we can do it ourselves.

———

There are writers who despise the dash. The sheer range of its use suggests that it's a lazy, all-purpose substitute for more disciplined forms of punctuation. Women seem to use it a lot, especially in correspondence, as if it were a woman's prerogative to stop short without explanation, to be a little vague, to have a sudden change of heart, to leave things open-ended. A friend of mine once swept aside all rules governing punctuation by saying, "Whenever you feel a pause, you put in a dash."

A reliance on dashes can feel breathless, but it can also be moving, as in this note that Jacqueline Kennedy wrote to Richard Nixon in response to his letter of condolence after the assassination of President Kennedy:

> I know how you must feel—so long on the path—so closely missing the greatest prize—and now for you, all the question comes up again—and you must commit all you and your family's and hopes and efforts again—Just one thing I would say to you—if it does not work out as you have hoped for so long—please be consoled by what you already have—your life and your family—

If a copy editor had standardized Jackie's punctuation, the note to Nixon would look like this:

I know how you must feel: so long on the path, so closely missing the greatest prize. And now, for you, all the question comes up again, and you must commit all you and your family's hopes and efforts again. Just one thing I would say to you: if it does not work out as you have hoped for so long, please be consoled by what you already have—your life and your family.

The conventionally punctuated version gives the prose the appearance of being tightly under control, buttons buttoned, snaps snapped, and jaw clamped shut. Jackie's dashes are spontaneous and expressive, full of style and personality. Dashes often comes in pairs, like commas or parentheses, and then they have to be coordinate; that is, after the second dash, the sentence has to pick up where it was suspended before the first dash. A sentence with more than two dashes can be ungainly, if not confusing. But in this case who cares if the dashes are not coordinate?

The most famous proponent of the dash was, of course, the poet Emily Dickinson, and it is because of her that, for me, the dash has a feminine slant. With Emily Dickinson at the table, my simplistic division of dashes into table forks and salad forks falls apart. She used dashes for everything, and sometimes for two things at once. If a different size and style of fork were assigned to each of her various dashes, the table setting would require not just dessert forks and fondue forks and those tiny forks used for teasing out snails but also tuning forks and pitchforks.

Dickinson's dashes have given rise to an entire academic industry. There is still no agreement among scholars over which of our conventional dashes suits her typographically. I think of dashes as an aid to conventional syntax, so I am not the ideal copy editor for, or even reader of, Emily Dickinson. The scholar Cristanne Miller writes, "In Dickinson's poetry the dash's primary function is rarely syntactic, to mark a tangential phrase for the reader or enclose a narrative aside. Rather, dashes typically isolate words for emphasis, provide a rhythmical syncopation to the meter and phrase of a line, and act as hooks on attention, slowing the reader's progress through the poem." Some scholars think the dashes were a form of musical notation, with the length of the dash indicating the length of the pause, or even a tonal system. R. W. Franklin, whose edition of the poems for Harvard University's Belknap Press is the approved academic text (there is both a single-volume "reading edition" and a three-volume variorum edition), writes that although the poet also used the comma and the period, she "relied mainly on dashes of varying length and position, tilting up or down as well as extending horizontally." While some of Dickinson's poems do have a period at the end, Miller writes that she "is apt to use the period ironically, to mock the expectation of final certainty." She is fond of the "syntactically ambiguous dash," which "both allows the sentence to continue (if we read the dash as dash) and makes the continuation a surprise (if we read the dash as end punctuation, which it often is in Dickinson's poetry)."

What is a copy editor to do? I don't hate ambiguity, but I can't be trusted to punctuate it, either. The one time it fell to me to style Dickinson's dashes, when her poetry was quoted in a book review by Judith Thurman, I blew it. The fact checker had on her desk the author's source, which had what I took for en dashes floating unmoored between the words. I'd never seen anything like this in *The New Yorker*. Quivering with impatience—

Patience - is the Smile's exertion
Through the quivering -

—I styled the verse in the most pedestrian way possible, marking
all the dashes as one ems and closing up the space between the
dash and the preceding word. The Library of America, in one of
its volumes of nineteenth-century American poetry, treats the
Dickinson dashes in this same flat-footed way. Today, the entire
archive of Emily Dickinson is available online, but even scholars who can read the poet's handwriting have to make decisions
about how to handle the dashes. In the Franklin edition, "a spaced
hyphen," as above, "rather than an en or an em dash, has been
used as appropriate to the relative weight of her dashes in most
of the poems." Franklin makes the point that Dickinson's poems
were never published by the poet herself. She copied her finished
poems onto sheets of folded stationery, poked holes in the fold,
and stitched them together, into what the scholars call fascicles.
So although poetry is "a public genre, to be brought editorially
into line with public norms of presentation," her poems should be
treated as a "private genre," like a letter or a diary, and therefore
her practice should be followed as closely as possible.

When Dickinson's pencil jottings on odds and ends of
paper—envelopes, receipts, wrapping paper—were published
as an art book, *The Gorgeous Nothings*, by Marta Werner and
Jen Bervin, I went downtown to see some of the originals in
an exhibit at the Drawing Center, in SoHo. They were under
glass and distorted by reflections from overhead lights, and it
was hard to inspect them without slobbering on the vitrine. An
artist friend who had been somewhat irritated by the show asked,
about Dickinson, "Didn't she have any pads of paper?" These

"Gorgeous Nothings" are not formal poems but things that the poet was thought to have been working up or fragments from her correspondence that she had decided to keep. Much is made of the way she fit them onto the scraps, some no bigger than a guitar pick. Of one vertical poem that begins "With Pinions of / Disdain," the scholar Susan Howe wrote that the dots over the *i*'s are expressive. Any poet who can get so much satisfaction out of dotting her *i*'s, as if concealing upside-down exclamation points of anger, deserves to have her dashes respected.

The dots and dashes actually put me in mind of telegrams, an obsolete form of communication (the Twitter of its time?) that had its own style—almost an anti-style—lacking any form of punctuation except the uninflected command "STOP."

———

There is no mark of punctuation so upper-crust as the semicolon. A writer friend who was born in England summed up her feelings for the semicolon in a remark worthy of Henry James: "There is no pleasure so acute as that of a well-placed semicolon." I guess the opposite of that is that there is no displeasure so obtuse as that of an ill-placed semicolon.

In my observation, the semicolon is used best by the British. I believe it's a matter of education, and that a classical education will feature a lot of semicolons, perhaps because they are needed to translate Latin and Greek. Americans can do without the semicolon, just as they can give Marmite a pass, with major exceptions: William and Henry James, as internationalists, were brought up on semicolons; Walt Whitman was into really long, ecstatic series, and the simplest use of the semicolon is as a kind of extra-strength comma to link items that have commas in them. Classics in America date only from the eighteenth century, and much of our best stuff comes out of Mark Twain and is in the vernacular. We are a plainspoken, cheerfully vulgar people. Which is not to say that Mark Twain couldn't or didn't use semicolons—only that Huck Finn would find them fancy.

I have a friend who worked as a copy editor in Canada, and whose education in Nova Scotia was more British than American. She is very fond of the semicolon, and uses it instead of a comma in the greeting of a letter, thus:

Dear Mary;

She swears that this is proper usage, that it was what she was taught and not her own innovation. She likes to think of the semicolon as a comma with vibrato. (She plays the viola.) I have never liked vibrato. I like a clear sound, without a lot of throb in it. Give me a comma or a period, period. Once in a while, when it is called for, a colon.

What is a semicolon, anyway? Is it half a colon? Is it a period balanced on top of a comma? The Italian for "semicolon" is *punto e virgola* ("period and comma"). Or an apostrophe that has been knocked down and pinned by a period? In Greek, both ancient and modern, what looks like a semicolon actually functions as a question mark. If you turn a semicolon upside down and hold it up to a mirror, it slightly resembles a question mark. I'll say this: as a copy editor, I find it the most pleasing mark to make. You have your caret, the upside-down *v* (∧) indicating that you want to insert something on the baseline, with a raised dot and a tail centered vertically beneath it.

In technical terms, the semicolon links independent clauses. This is wrong:

"It ends a clause; and it links a clause to the clause before."

This is right:

"It ends a clause; it links a clause to the clause before."

This is also right:

"It ends a clause, and it links a clause to the clause before."

The semicolon can be done without. You can substitute a comma and a conjunction. But our system of punctuation is highly economical, and if the semicolon has survived all this time there must be some reason for it.

The thing about the semicolon is that, unless it is being used in the Whitmanesque sense, what follows it must be able to function as its own sentence—an independent clause. The semicolon creates a hook on which to dangle something off the first part of the sentence. It irritates me when someone uses the semicolon to join things that really have no relation to each other; it is a bald maneuver to make you keep reading. I see the semicolon a lot more than I used to, either because I'm reading more British writers or because American writers have British editors or because American writers are competing with British writers to show that they, too, are sophisticated. Used well, the semicolon makes a powerful impression; misused, it betrays your ignorance.

You can open a volume of Henry James at random and find numerous well-tempered semicolons. I picked up *The Henry James Reader*, edited by Leon Edel. This is from *The Aspern Papers*:

"You must wait—you must wait," Miss Tina mournfully moralised; and her tone ministered little to my patience, for it seemed after all to accept that wretched possibility. I would teach myself to wait, I declared nevertheless; because in the first place I couldn't do otherwise and in the second I had her promise, given me the other night, that she would help me.

"Of course if the papers are gone that's no use," she said; not as if she wished to recede, but only to be conscientious.

"Naturally. But if you could only find out!" I groaned, quivering again.

These semicolons don't exactly follow modern conventions, and the ones that are combined with conjunctions could be replaced with commas, but something would be lost. James's semicolons are like Melville's commas, raised to a higher degree: the pauses seem to indicate facial expressions—raised eyebrows, pursed lips, a puckered brow. They heighten the prose.

In James, the semicolon is often followed by a conjunction that shouldn't be necessary. From *Washington Square*:

She *was* bad; but she couldn't help it.

Eleanor Gould had a rule about these things: a semicolon could not follow a dash. The dash was too fragile to hold it up. Henry James did not follow Gould. For example:

Poor Catherine was conscious of her freshness; it gave her a feeling about the future which rather added to the weight upon her mind. It seemed a proof that she was strong and solid and dense, and would live to a great age—longer than might be generally convenient; and this idea was pressing, for it appeared to saddle her with a pretension the more, just when the cultivation of any pretension was inconsistent with her doing right.

Is not that semicolon after "generally convenient" priceless? Like Emily Dickinson with her dashes, Henry James uses semicolons for timing. They accumulate in a way that can make sentiments feel simultaneous, although it's impossible to read two things at once. It's like a trio in opera.

James also proves wrong my objection to semicolons in dialogue. The Doctor, in *Washington Square*, to Aunt Penniman (his sister):

"You have taken up young Townsend; that's your own affair. I have nothing to do with your sentiments, your fancies, your affections, your delusions; but what I request of you is that you will keep these things to yourself. I have explained my views to Catherine; she understands them perfectly, and anything that she does further in the way of encouraging Mr. Townsend's attentions will be in deliberate opposition to my wishes."

Mrs. Penniman replies, "It seems to me you talk like a great autocrat."

She means, of course, that what he says is cruel and authoritarian, but the semicolons and the cadences they create help form those pinions of disdain. The carefully calculated punctuation is perfectly in character. If James used more pedestrian punctuation, the Doctor would not sound so tyrannical; he would come across as cavalier.

I wouldn't change a semicolon of James's any more than I would meddle with the space around a dash of Emily Dickinson's. Each little piece of punctuation is calibrated for its effect and pressed into the service of an exquisite sensibility.

———

In the hierarchy of punctuation marks, as set forth by Eleanor Gould, a dash can follow a colon or a semicolon, but a colon or a semicolon cannot follow a dash (unless the dash is one of a coordinated pair). The logic is that the stronger mark controls the weaker; the weaker cannot contain the stronger. It sounds like a copy editor's scheme for world domination, but it makes a certain amount of sense.

A colon is a very controlling gesture. It says, "Right this way," like a proper butler. A sentence should have only one colon, just as it should have only one period. A butler would never tolerate another butler in the same household. Though a colon can sometimes be replaced by a dash, the colon is more formal. For instance, the following sentence has a pair of coordinate dashes and an eloquent colon before the last clause: "Unable to visit Bruichladdich—unable, anymore, even to enjoy its whisky—Reynier devised a modest plan to save his favorite spirit: he would buy the distillery." I had never noticed before how much Kelefa Sanneh, writing about Scotch, can sound like Henry James.

A colon is sometimes preferable to a semicolon if the thrust of the sentence is forward: you are amplifying something, providing a definition or a list or an illustration. The semicolon sets up a different relationship; whatever follows relates in a more subtle way to what came before. A dash can perform either of these services, but it is looser, less formal. In Dickens, for instance, I went looking for some of the doubled-up punctuation marks that the Victorians had a penchant for, what Nicholson Baker calls "dashtards": the commash (,—) and the colash (:—) and the semicolash (;—). In his letters, Dickens also used the stopdash (.—). Seeing them here, enclosed in parentheses, I marvel at their resemblance to emoticons. Instead of building emoticons out of punctuation marks ((((:>)), the Victorians built emotions into their punctuation.

In Dickens I discovered something unexpected: an abundance of double dashes—two-em dashes, closed up. "Gaffer! If you think to get rid of me this way——" He uses the double dash in dialogue, to convey an interruption compounded by a threat. The double dash is strangely expressive, packing an extra dose of suspense, as if the speaker, rendered inarticulate by emotion, were resorting to his fists. And, when you think about it, suspense is what punctuation is all about: how is the author going to finish the sentence?

Chapter 8
....

WHAT'S UP WITH THE
APOSTROPHE?

THE WORD "APOSTROPHE" GOES BACK to Greek drama. A
"strophe," or "turn," meant a stanza in a Greek choral ode—
the chorus sang and danced in one direction. The strophe was
followed by an "antistrophe," or "turn against," when the chorus whipped around in the other direction, and sang lyrics in
response to the first stanza. "Apostrophe" means "turn from,"
and refers to a rhetorical device in which the actor turns from
the action and addresses someone or something who is not there.
"Apostrophe" still has this meaning in English, and "apostrophize" has become a verb. I first encountered it in *The Innocents
Abroad*, when Mark Twain observes his fellow tourists gawking
at Leonardo's *Last Supper*, in Milan: "You would think that those
men had an astonishing talent for seeing things that had already
passed away. It was what I thought when I stood before 'The
Last Supper' and heard men apostrophizing wonders and beau-

ties and perfections which had faded out of the picture and gone a hundred years before they were born." From this, I thought "to apostrophize" meant "to praise," and I honestly can't tell whether the emphasis is on the rapture of the tourists or on the nonexistence of what they were enraptured by. An apostrophe is almost like a prayer, when a prayer comes from the impulse to praise.

And the apostrophe is going to need our prayers if it is to survive in its approved form. There are real questions about the use of the apostrophe in a possessive. For instance, which side of the *s* does it go on in "farmer's market"? I prefer "farmers' market," assuming that there is more than one farmer. Some people insist that "hornet's nest" is the proper form, though there is more than one hornet. I once asked Eleanor Gould how to make the plural possessive of McDonald's, and she very sensibly told me to leave it alone. "You have to stop somewhere," she said. We stopped at McDonald'ses'.

And yet commercial enterprises with faulty apostrophes have produced some success stories. Barneys New York, the high-end clothing store, was founded by Barney Pressman, a purveyor of men's discount clothing, as Barney's, in 1923; it dropped the apostrophe in 1979, at the behest of Gene Pressman, the grandson of Barney, who introduced a line of very expensive women's clothing, and the enterprise took off, as copy editors, bereft of the apostrophe and unable to afford the clothes, gnashed their teeth. Gary Comer, a native of Chicago, worked for ten years as a copywriter at Young & Rubicam before dropping out to bum around Europe, where, in the Swiss Alps, he read *The Magic Mountain*, whose feverish young hero made him contemplate "whether there would be life after 33, and what it might consist of." When he went home, he and some friends decided to live life to the fullest by making a living off their love of sailing, and opened a mail-order company specializing in nautical goods. They named it Land's End, after the fabled westernmost tip of Cornwall. On the cover of their first catalogue, in 1963, Land's End appeared as Lands' End, a truly fabulous place. The company couldn't afford to reprint the catalogue, and the misplaced apostrophe did not prevent Comer from becoming a billionaire.

Apostrophes seem to be always on the move. I used to think the loss of the apostrophe in place-names was a natural process, a form of linguistic erosion. You see it all the time in New York: the Bronx was once owned by Jonas Bronck: Bronck's farm—the Bronx. Queens was claimed by the British in the name Catherine of Braganza; that land was the Queen's—Queens. Rikers Island, Wards Island, and Randalls Island were named for Riker, Ward, and Randall. St. Marks Place, home of head shops and tattoo parlors, was named for St. Mark's-in-the-Bouwerie, New York's oldest continuously operating center of worship, which retains its hyphens.

For years, I have gone with friends to a certain island in Lake Erie for a writers' retreat, and I am always careful to spell the name of the island as it appears on the ferry: Kelleys Island. My friends, well-educated people, sometimes give it an apostrophe, writing Kelley's Island, and sometimes misspell it, too: Kelly's Island. Together we have poked around in the island cemetery, where you cannot miss the obelisk that commemorates the Kelley family. Originally, there were two of them on the island, brothers, Datus and Irad, immigrants from Connecticut. Kelleys Island was part of Connecticut's Western Reserve, which at one time stretched all the way to the Pacific. The surveyors named it Island No. 6. Eventually, the Kelleys bought up every plot on the island, and developed its natural resources, which consisted mostly of fish (perch and walleye) and limestone. They also grew grapes and made wine, but, in my opinion, they needn't have bothered with the wine.

As it happens, Kelleys Island presents a paradigm of apostrophe use. If, say, Datus Kelley had coveted his brother Irad's share of the land and slain him with a large chunk of the island's indigenous limestone, leaving just one Kelley, the island would properly have been called Kelley's Island, with an apostrophe plus *s*. Because there were two Kelley brothers and they shared the island, fishing and quarrying and winemaking, the island was named after both Kelleys, the plural being formed the regular way, by adding an *s*, and the possessive by hanging an apostrophe onto the end: Kelleys' Island. Easy. An apostrophe *s* may sound the same as an *s* used to form a plural, but not for us what Fowler calls a "fatuous vulgarism." The Kelleys are long gone—the Kelley Mansion, the showplace of the island, is now owned by a guy named Lemley, who sits on the porch in overalls and charges two dollars for a tour. As the plural form of a proper noun, Kelleys can be used as an attributive: Kelleys limestone, like Beatles music or Carrara marble. Well, maybe not so much like Carrara marble.

Anyway, that was how I justified the lack of an apostrophe in Kelleys Island. It's not as if there weren't legions of stray apostrophes camping out on the island. There is a store called Village Tee's, meaning, I suppose, T-shirts (or golf tees?) of the Village, unless it belongs to someone who goes by the name Village Tee. In front of a store on the way to the glacial grooves, an outcropping of stone scarred from the last ice age, is a reader board with the letters arranged to say "UNC'L DIK'S." There are so many things wrong with "UNC'L DIK'S" that I don't know where to begin, but at least the apostrophe *s* at the end is right. I'm guessing that Uncle Dick bought an alphabet with only one of each letter, so he decided to distribute the *C* and the *K* equally between the elements of his name. He may have dropped the *E* in the lake, but he made up for it with an extra apostrophe.

Many of the houses on Kelleys Island have signs out front with the house's name on them. One sign says "Our Secret Hide-away," and I always think, Not anymore. Many announce the name of the family that owns the house, saying something like "Volt's" when it should say just "Volt" or "The Volts'" (unless there is only one old Volt holed up in there, in which case it seems unlikely that he would advertise). If you are going to put a sign with your family's name on it in front of your house, as if to say "Our House," then you want the plural possessive: The Volts'. And if your name ends in an *s* you still want the plural, even if it looks terrible: The Norrises'. And if you don't like it, simply refrain from putting a sign with your name on it in front of your house. And if someone else buys a custom-made sign for you with a mistake on it, the dump is on Dump Road, off Bookerman, in the center of the island.

All my ruminations on the name Kelleys Island turned out to be in vain. Kelleys Island did not suffer from apostrophe erosion— it had the apostrophe legislated out of it. The same is true of Harpers Ferry and Pikes Peak and Snedens Landing and St. Marks Place. In 1906, Teddy Roosevelt instructed a government body called the U.S. Board on Geographic Names, started by Benjamin Harrison in 1890, to begin standardizing place-names, and the board determined that "the word or words that form a geographic name" undergo a change, losing the original meaning and becoming "fixed labels used to refer to geographic entities." By official government policy, "the need to imply possession or association no longer exists." Therefore the United States has what Barry Newman, in the *Wall Street Journal,* called "an apostrophe-eradication policy." (The apostrophes in Irish names like O'Malley and O'Connor have been grandfathered in.) Martha's Vineyard had its apostrophe restored in 1933, after almost four decades of deprivation. It has the eighth-oldest surviving place-name in the country, and, as with spelling in general, the name has history in it. Not that anyone is clear what that history is. The *Vineyard Gazette* traces the name back to 1602 and the English explorer Bartholomew Gosnold, who may have named the island for his daughter Martha, who lies buried in Bury St. Edmonds, formerly St. Edmond's Bury, in Suffolk, England.

———

Are we losing the apostrophe? Is it just too much trouble? This little squiggle, so like a comma except that it has been hoisted up above the letters instead of hooked below the baseline, comes to us through French, which has many words that slide together. (*Qu'est-ce que c'est?*) Gertrude Stein, who had no use for commas and hated the question mark, had a weakness for the apostrophe. In "Poetry and Grammar," she wrote that "for some the possessive case apostrophe has a gentle tender insinuation that makes it very difficult to definitely decide to do without."

Probably we should not rely on Gertrude Stein, however, if the idea is to write clearly. The apostrophe has two uses in English:

it forms the possessive, as so sweetly renounced by Ms. Stein, and it papers over contractions, closing up a gap in a word where a letter or letters have dropped out: can't, won't, don't, ain't; o'clock; Chock full o'Nuts; rock 'n' roll (if you must); po'boy (if you want an oyster sandwich instead of an indigent youth). Neither of these functions elevates the apostrophe to the rank of a true mark of punctuation: it changes the form of a word without indicating a pause or a stop or an intonation or having any effect at the level of the sentence. Like the blank in a game of Scrabble (if Scrabble allowed contractions or possessives), it fills in for a missing letter. But for various reasons this subtle signal is under attack.

Something there is in cyberspace that doesn't love an apostrophe. It is scorned in domain names. The GPS does not recognize it. In England, home of the Apostrophe Protection Society, there was a big flap in 2013, when the Mid-Devon District Council banned the apostrophe in certain place-names "to avoid 'confusion.'" It would have affected the signs for Beck's Square, Blundell's Avenue, and St. George's Well. One Mary de Vere Taylor, a proofreader from Ashburton, said that "the thought of apostrophes being removed made her shudder. . . . 'Some may say I should get a life and get out more but if I got out more and saw place names with no apostrophes where there should be I shudder to think how I'd react.'"

With the advent of texting, there is less will to insist on the apostrophe, even in contractions. People are lazy, and it's a pain to have to switch screens, from letters to symbols and back again, in order to type "I'll" instead of letting the phone take over and write "ill." I like apostrophes, but I am continually frustrated by the ready-made forms that my smartphone throws up. Contractions are less formal in speech, but if they're cumbersome to type either the apostrophe will disappear or the contraction will become two words again.

In the end, the Mid-Devon council backed down. It never meant to do away with the apostrophe entirely, or suggest that the rules governing it were so confusing that we might as well give up. It's not rocket science. But the GPS bounces off satellites—it *is* rocket science—and no one had programmed into it *Eats, Shoots and Leaves,* the 2003 best-seller in which Lynne Truss sorted out the possessive ("the British government's idea") from the plural ("the ideas of governments on both sides of the Atlantic") and the plural possessive ("all governments' stupid ideas"). The three Mid-Devonian apostrophes were saved, at least for now. The Apostrophe Protection Society rejoiced, and linguists snickered to think that people really thought they couldn't do without the apostrophe or even considered it a mark of punctuation.

————

Although the Apostrophe Protection Society was founded "with the specific aim of preserving the correct use of this currently much abused punctuation mark in all forms of text written in the English language," its Web site consists chiefly of a running list of apostrophic abominations: "Taxi's Only"; "Don't Judge a Book by It's Movie"; "Ladie's," "Vice-Chancellors Lodge Private Grounds"; "Toilette's Are for Customer's Use." The more one looks at bad apostrophes, the more familiar they grow and the more acceptable they seem. The chairman of the APS is a retired "subeditor," which is what they call a copy editor in England. His work consisted largely of "adding, deleting or moving apostrophes," and even once he retired he couldn't stop. Great sport is made of what Lynne Truss calls the grocer's apostrophe, a sort of poor relation of the Oxford comma. I could go across the street to the grocery store and be almost certain of seeing a sign—printed, not hand-lettered—that said "Banana's" or "Papaya's." The chief problem is that, in the interests of economy, the language has pressed into service the letter *s* for two different purposes: to form the plural and, in combination with the apostrophe, to make a noun into a possessive adjective. Sometimes these functions overlap or get confused, and someone uses the apostrophe to form the plural. Is that ground for despair? The APS states on its site, "We are aware of the way the English language is evolving during use, and do not intend any direct criticism of those who have made mistakes, but are just reminding all writers of English text, whether on notices or in documents of any type, of the correct usage of the apostrophe should you wish to put right any mistakes you may have inadvertently made."

I don't know if Eleanor Gould was invited to join the APS, but she would have approved of it. Lu Burke, on the other hand, would have thought that a retired copy editor should have better things to do than continue to chase down errant bits of punctuation. When she retired, the folks in Heritage Village, up in Connecticut, asked whether she was interested in proofreading their newsletter. She turned them down. Apostrophes and whatnot could worry about themselves.

Why should a grocer have to master apostrophes, anyway? Things that are correct disappear, in a good way, while things that are incorrect can sometimes amuse. In Times Square I saw a sign that said "STREET CLOSEURE," a touch of French that gives our American thoroughfares some class. Maybe the typo that appeared in the name Jesus on a commemorative gold coin issued by the Vatican—"LESUS"—was Jesus' way of saying, "Don't waste God's money on commemorative gold coins." The lunch specials chalked on a blackboard outside a restaurant in the East Village included a "salomon snad." I would never order a salmon sandwich—doesn't sound good; obviously, it's not sushi-grade salmon if they're making patties out of it—but I found the salomon snad quite beguiling.

Think of apostrophes as jewelry—maybe that's what would make us handle them properly. The apostrophe is possessive: it will hang in.

Chapter 9
....

F*CK THIS SH*T

H AS THE CASUAL USE OF profanity in English reached a high
tide? That's a rhetorical question, but I'm going to answer it
anyway: Fuck yeah.

In some ways, it's a beautiful thing. Jon Stewart, on *The Daily
Show,* is so gleeful in his use of every raunchy variation on the
seven words George Carlin said you couldn't say on TV or radio
("fuck," "piss," "shit," "cunt," "motherfucker," "cocksucker," and "tits")
that he seems set jubilantly free. Of course, censorship has come
a long way, too. The bleep master leaves just enough snippet of
syllable to add mirth to such colorful expressions as "you dairy-
aisle motherfbleepking bleep." In the English-speaking world,
uncensored profanity probably reaches its apogee on the British
series *The Thick of It,* written by Armando Ianucci (with "swear-
ing consultant" Ian Martin), follows a ruthless political operative
who cannot put two syllables together without wedging a curse
in between. "E-fucking-nough," he says. "Fuckety-bye." In puri-

tanical America, by contrast, prime-time shows are accessorized with asterisks, dashes, and euphemisms: *S*** My Father Says, Don't Trust the B——— in Apartment 23, It's Effin' Science.* I like to think that the person who blew it all open was Richard Nixon, back in the seventies, with his [expletives deleted] on the Watergate tapes—insomuch as it has been blown open. (Did anyone ever print the president's actual words?) The *New York Times* persists in stifling the "common barnyard epithet," even when a book titled *On Bullshit*—a work of philosophy by a scholar at Yale—appeared on its best-seller list, in 2005. There is a blog devoted to the *Times*'s runarounds (fit-to-print) and a perennial argument between reporters and editors over what should be quoted directly and what should be waltzed around, and why. Whose delicate sensibilities are we catering to? Certainly not mine—not anymore.

It is important in any discussion of bad language to separate blasphemy from cursing. Nobody is advocating breaking the second commandment, "Thou shalt not take the name of the Lord thy God in vain," though, admittedly, it's sometimes a challenge. Whatever you may say about the G-d of the Old Testament, he does not seem to have had much sense of humor. I mean, Jesus! According to Moses, Yahweh put "Thou shalt not kill" way down the list of commandments, at No. 5, but already at No. 2 he is abjuring us not to have any fun at his expense? I was in a church shortly after Hurricane Sandy, in the fall of 2012, when someone asked the priest how his congregation had fared during the storm. He answered that in Brooklyn Heights all was well but that his brethren in Dumbo had suffered bad flooding. "Oh, God!" I said—and then tried to inhale it back. Here I was in church, and I couldn't think of any better way to register sympathy? I might have said "What a pity" or "God have mercy on the poor souls Down Under the Manhattan Bridge Overpass." But these are not expressions that spring readily to mind, whereas the mild oath popped out right there in front of the tabernacle, like an egg I was helpless not to lay. I hoped that it might pass as a brief prayer.

I cannot help but admire, in retrospect, the restraint shown by my father as I was growing up. The strongest thing I ever heard him say when something went wrong—for instance, during a plumbing project, when the ceramic sink he was installing shattered into a thousand pieces—was "You dog." Still, the way he said it, you knew that he was not invoking just any old household pet. Sometimes he said "Great Scott" or, when he was feeling especially vehement, "Great Scott Murgatroyd." He was a fireman, and was scandalized once, responding to an alarm backstage at the Cleveland Play House, to hear Lauren Bacall, whom he admired—a lot—curse at the firemen for barging into her dressing room. He had never heard a woman say "fuck" (if that is what Ms. Bacall said; I'm sure she didn't stammer at the firemen, "You . . . *words!*"). I certainly never heard *him* say "fuck"—not until he tried to drive in New Jersey.

My mother, on the other hand, was a font of vulgarity, a regular gusher. She would as soon call the neighbors assholes as tell them to mind their own business. Her epithet of choice for our nosy aunt was Fuzz Nuts. And she had vivid ideas about where her enemies might pound salt. When I took a course on Aristophanes in the original Greek I was reminded of my mother. I did not have a big enough Greek-English lexicon to translate a lot of the words in *Peace*, so I would go to Columbia's Butler Library to use the huge Liddell & Scott, and I swear every other word I looked up in this temple of academe turned out to mean "fart." I worried that when it was my turn to translate in class, I might, channeling my mother, say something so dirty it would have embarrassed Aristophanes.

I never cursed much myself until I was well into adulthood. I uttered a decorous little "crap" once, slamming my locker door in high school. I was saving the hard stuff for later. My friends and I went to see the movie *Butch Cassidy and the Sundance Kid* over and over, and never failed to laugh at the scene when Robert Redford admits to Paul Newman that he can't swim, but, to escape their trackers, he jumps off the cliff into the river anyway, bellowing "SHHHHHIIIIIIIIITTTT" on the way down.

In college, the upperclassmen talked about "getting their shit together"; we got "shit-faced" on Coke and Southern Comfort; "good shit" was excellent weed. One friend became worried when she realized that "fuck" was her default response to anything. If a little old lady on the bus started telling my friend her troubles, she found herself replying, "Fuck." The old lady could be forgiven for not knowing that in context—a university town in New Jersey in the early seventies—"fuck" could mean "I'm sorry to hear that." I first gave full vent to the urge to curse after terminating analysis, in 1996. I felt so free—I could change jobs, move from Queens to Manhattan, enjoy a little discretionary income because I wasn't always shelling out to the shrink—and I just let fly with every joyous expletive I could think of. If someone mentioned *The House of Mirth*, I would say, "Edith Wharton blows," or if a friend suggested reading *Middlemarch* my response was "George Eliot sucks." It was so satisfying. The shell of prudery surrounding childhood and adolescence cracked wide open, and I emerged a fucking monarch butterfly. So I would say that analysis worked for me.

And yet in this climate it can be so fucking hard to keep your equilibrium. In the spring of 2012, *The New Yorker* ran a piece by Kelefa Sanneh about the rapper Earl Sweatshirt, whose mother sent him to reform school in Samoa because he had fallen in with bad companions. After reading the piece seven or eight times, making sure that "Shit sucks" and "OMG Fucking Just Ran From A Pack Of Fans Threw Coachella. Shit Was Wild!" and "LETS SWAG IT OUT" were rendered exactly as they were in the video or the tweet, I was so disoriented that I stetted a big-ass mistake at the end. What was the point of making a fuss over a "than" for a "then" in a piece so full of profanity, especially if that's what the kid wrote? There should be a detox facility for proofreaders who have undergone this kind of extreme experience. I have never fully recovered my judgment and can no longer be trusted to distinguish a true, pithy utterance from a gratuitous four-letter word.

At the time, I did not know that there was an informal contest going on at the magazine to see which writer could get the most instances of "fuck" into print, and that Sanneh was going head to head with the editor of *The New Yorker* himself, David Remnick, for the title. You can't write about rappers or about boxing without quoting a few obscenities, and if you are fluent in Russian, as Remnick is, you have a whole world of obscenities at your fingertips. In Russia there is an underground language called *mat*, loosely analogous to rap, in that it was first spoken on the street and in jail, and it puts Russophiles way out in front. As Remnick summarizes it, all of *mat* is based on four words: "there is *khuy* ('cock'), *pizda* ('cunt'), *ebat'* ('to fuck'), and *blyad* ('whore')." Victor

Erofeyev went into startling lingustic detail in a *New Yorker* piece. "The term *mat* itself dervies from the Russian word for 'mother,' a component of the key phrase *yob tveyu mat'* ('fuck your mother')," Erofeyev wrote. A flexible system of prefixes and suffixes makes it possible to twist and build the four words into an incredible variety of obscene shapes. Peter the Great, Dostoyevsky, Push-kin, Lermontov—all made use of *khuy* and *ebat'*. One of the milder expressions cited by Erofeyev, *khuem grushi okolachivat*—an equiv-alent of the beautiful Italian idiom *dolce far niente*—translates as "knocking pears out of a tree with one's dick."

It is as if *The New Yorker* had developed a raging case of Tourette's syndrome since the days when Pauline Kael fought constantly with William Shawn to get the word "shit" into print. Kael was on leave in the late summer of 1979, when *Apocalypse Now* came out, and Mr. Shawn let Veronica Geng, who was filling in as movie critic, quote the opening lines: "Saigon. Shit." Kael had missed her opportunity. Years earlier, Calvin Trillin, cover-ing the desegregation of schools in the South, had determined to resign in protest if Shawn did not agree to print the exact words spoken by Lester Maddox, the governor of Georgia: "The federal government could take its education money and 'ram it.'" Shawn ultimately agreed that the specific words were germane to the story. Robert Gottlieb carried on the conservative tradition when he decided not to let John McPhee quote sailors saying what sail-ors actually say in a report about a merchant marine. McPhee got his satisfaction years later in a piece about editors when he simply turned on the tap and filled a paragraph with "fuck"s.

The generation of writers who were hired by Shawn in the mid-seventies to write for Talk of the Town were often puz-zled by some of his prohibitions. In addition to the usual bodily fluids—piss, shit, blood, and spit—he was squeamish about fish hooks, wigs, twins, and midgets. Mark Singer once had a reference to Ex-Lax removed from a story about the dirty-tricks campaign for state senator of Roy Goodman, whose family money came from Ex-Lax. And in a story tabulating the cost of taking the subway to a movie and buying refreshments, the editors cut Junior Mints. When Singer asked why, the style editor, Hobie Weekes, told him, "A *New Yorker* writer should not be eating Junior Mints." According to Ian Frazier, the sentence incorporating as many Shawn taboos as possible was "The short, balding man wearing a wig took his menstruating wife to a boxing match."

But by now the pendulum has swung to the other side. Frazier, who, not incidentally, studied Russian for his travels in Siberia, wrote a piece for a magazine produced by the Russian artist Alex Melamid, the *Rubber Band Society Gazette*, which was basically a page covered with obscenities. Remnick "said he liked it," Frazier recalled, "and that emboldened me to do one for him." Thus was born the Cursing Mommy, a sort of Heloise whose hints veer into rants with lines like "Somebody please tell me I have not lost my stupid goddam fucking drink." She uses a vacuum cleaner called the SukMore. Thanks to the Cursing Mommy, Frazier was able to claim, "I've put more curse words on a single page of *The New Yorker* than anyone."

My sense of what is truly profane—what is fun and what is journalism—has been untrustworthy since the Earl Sweatshirt incident. When Ben McGrath, writing about a soccer team in Brazil, used the phrase "bros before hos," my first concern was the spelling of "hos." I might have been distracted by the Portuguese—it is the only language I've ever studied that brought me to tears. I used the universal search to put the accent over the *a* in "São Paulo," and insisted that for *real*, the Brazilian monetary unit, we use the Portuguese plural, *reais*. (In Portuguese, *r* is pronounced like *h*, and *l* like *w*, so *real* is pronounced hey-ow and *reais* is hey-ice.) That accent in *ão* represents a nasalized diphthong that sounds like a prehistoric bird uncorking its love call. Mispronounced—and it is virtually impossible for foreigners to pronounce correctly (except certain prodigies from Flint, Michigan)—it will make you a laughingstock in the bakery: you think you're asking for a loaf of bread (*pão*) but are actually demanding wood (*pao*), which in Portuguese, as in English, is a variant on "dick."

Anyway, in context, "bros before hos" referred to soccer players on a bus when one of them wanted time off to spend with his new girlfriend; in a display of "bros before hos" camaraderie, he was denied. The second reader on the piece circled "new girlfriend" and "hos" and wrote, "synonymous?" Well, of course they weren't synonymous. I did not take the query seriously. I was still bent on making sure no one confused "hos" with "hoes," the garden implement. It came up again in the closing meeting: "Is it really OK to print this?" the writer asked. I mentioned my colleague's qualm—he is a jock, and he is married, and he wouldn't want his wife to see herself dismissed as a ho. Still, I thought that in context it was clearly not serious—it was lighthearted, a reference to guys talking trash. So we left it in.

The piece was no sooner published than someone tweeted about *The New Yorker*'s first use of "bros before hos." Of course. The contest now is more about being the first to get into print an obscenity that has not been used by anyone else. Then a story broke in the Brazilian press—something about a soccer team being compared with a whorehouse—and I realized that those soccer players and their wives and girlfriends would naturally be interested in what was being written about them and would ask someone to translate it for them. How would "bros before hos" come out in Portuguese? Would it be something like "players versus prostitutes"? Had we inadvertently compared a soccer team to a whorehouse? I spent a terrible day and night thinking about those players and their wives and girlfriends and how the women would be outraged at being called whores, and all the wives would boycott the sport and the controversy would reach the president of Brazil, Dilma Rousseff, who is a woman, and it would become an international incident, with Brazil denying entry to American journalists. Brazil is a Catholic country, and although soccer is not above violence and vulgar insults (there was an anecdote in the piece about a player who had posed kissing another man, to show his support for gays; the fans called him a faggot at the next game), maybe it's not so funny for a woman to casually be called a hooker. I had been careless. I never stopped to think how a bit of American slang would sound translated into Portuguese. Then again do you always have to stop and think how something is going to sound in Portuguese?

Sports often raise such dilemmas, where you have to choose between reporting a crude thing someone said and reflecting that maybe this isn't actually news. It turned out that what had excited comment in Brazil was not the "bros before hos" line but something a Brazilian had actually said in the piece—a direct quotation, in English, in which the vice-president of a soccer team compared running the team to being in charge of a whorehouse, and loving it. Because it was in a quotation, it did not occur to me to query it, even though I couldn't quite believe what I was reading. So I stopped worrying about having caused an international incident. "Bros before hos" produced a letter from an irate reader in Milwaukee, who thought the usage demonstrated casual misogyny and made me realize that my job had been to support the writer, who had expressed doubt about using the phrase. Mea culpa.

In another demonstration of impaired judgment, I read a piece in which an executive in charge of an important group recalled saying to his critics, "Fuck you!" I thought, That's harsh. But I didn't suggest changing it. The reporter was scrupulous, and the executive had been quoted accurately. I had a chance to query it again on the second round—a second chance to have second thoughts. But again I told myself that this executive obviously didn't care what anyone thought. When I read the piece one last time, the "Fuck you" was gone. At the closing meeting, the editor made some reference to ultimately deciding to take the profanity out. Had I again shown a lapse in judgment by not querying a profanity? And if I hadn't queried it, who had? And did whoever queried it think I was not doing my job? Had the writer and the editor just been waiting for me to take it out? Was I like a parent who should be setting limits? I found myself relieved once it was gone, and that relief, more than anything else, made me realize that I should have queried it.

I followed up on this incident with the editor and found out that it was the executive who objected to being quoted saying something so forceful, so bridge-burning and provocative— and in the boardroom, no less. The editor described himself as "merciless," inclined always to go ahead with the verbatim quotation and let the subject live with it: "If you said it, you said it—you can't take it back now." But the executive explained that he had been paraphrasing himself. This one instance of the word's being withheld was more instructive than all the times the word was printed. It showed that it still had force.

————

Every once in a while, the power of the euphemism asserts itself. "Euphemism" is another word with Greek roots: *eu*, good (as in "eugenics," good genes, or "utopia," good place, as spelled by Thomas More), and *pheme*, something spoken. It means a sugar-coating. "Fiddlesticks" is Scarlett O'Hara's way of saying "Fuck this shit." "Phooey" might be Shirley Temple's preference. "Jeepers" and "Jiminy Cricket" are variations on "Jesus" and "Jesus Christ." I have spent whole hangover days laughing at the idea of a law firm with letterhead stationery printed "Johnson, Johnson, Johnson & Johnson." I don't know why it took me so long to find the name of the Band-Aid and baby-shampoo company in my college town funny: New Brunswick's own Johnson & Johnson. I am sure that Samuel Johnson, the father of lexicography, would get a kick out of knowing that his surname was synonymous with penis. One day, in the course of my mundane working life, I read the words "Robert Caro writes in the most recent volume of his Johnson biography . . ." and cracked up. I know that Caro is writing the definitive biography of Lyndon B. Johnson, but in the privacy of my office I permitted myself to picture Robert Caro as a square-looking guy who had yet led a life of such sexual adventurism that he needed to write a multivolume biography of his Johnson.

I'm not sure how much further we can take profanity and still enjoy it. The lexicographer Jesse Sheidlower edited *The F-Word*, a 270-page alphabetized collection of variations on this versatile oath. My colleagues and I have argued in the office over whether it should be rendered F-word, F word, "F" word, or "f" word, but who really gives a fuck about the proper form of a euphemism? It is an odd thing to strive to be consistent about. Downstairs at the Strand, New York's legendary used-book store, in the section on language, various editions of Sheidlower's lexicon take up a few feet on the miles of shelves. My own copy is a late edition, a sleek red hardcover, but when *The F-Word* first came out, in 1995, it was packaged as if wrapped in plain brown paper, like pornography. *The F-Word* is a little bit like the Rock and Roll Hall of Fame: a dictionary, like a museum exhibit, is bound to deprive the thing it enshrines of the raw quality that gave it its vitality in the first place.

You cannot legislate language. Prohibition never worked, right? Not for booze and not for sex and not for words. And yet no one wants to be pummeled constantly by four-letter words. If we are going to use them, let's use them right. Profanity ought to be fun. I love the title of this chapter and thought I should spell out those words uncensored—swag it out! But I like it even better with the blessed euphemism: the asterisks standing in for the vowels are interior punctuation, little fireworks inside the words.

Chapter 10
....

BALLAD OF A
PENCIL JUNKIE

A S A CHILD, I HAD two formative experiences with pencils. The first was in kindergarten, when we were learning to print our names. We were sitting in miniature chairs at low tables, and the teacher, Miss Crosby, had put a card in front of each of us with our name printed on it, and we were supposed to practice copying our name onto a sheet of paper. I clutched the thick Ticonderoga, and though I formed each letter with great care, when I was finished and sat back to behold the finished product, it was gibberish: sirroN yraM. Miss Crosby came up behind me (I didn't like that; those were the days of bomb shelters and air-raid drills, and you never knew what might happen) and moved my right hand—the one with the pencil in it—to the far side of the sheet of paper, and when I copied my name again it came unscrambled. For years after that, to get started on the right—that is, the left—side of the paper I had to close my eyes and transport myself back to that kindergarten classroom, with the blocks and the beads and the yellow stains on the floor, and picture the door in back of me and the tall windows in front of me, and then move my hand across my body in the direction of the window farthest from the door, and place the pencil on the paper. That is how I learned to write from left to right.

The other experience took place at home, at the kitchen table. My parents had "stepped out," as my mother said—they did this very rarely, going down to a beer joint called the Ivy Inn on Denison Avenue—and left my brother Miles in charge. I was amusing myself with pencil and paper. I liked to lick the tip of the pencil lead before applying it to the paper. I suppose I imagined that a moistened pencil point made a darker impression. This was a different kind of pencil—I had scraped it up from somewhere, possibly from my father's workbench. There was a chronic shortage of pencils in our house. It had no eraser on top, and its mark was purplish. It was especially satisfying to lick. Miles noticed what I was doing, and said, "That's an indelible pencil!" My hands were stained and my lips were blue. He told me to stick out my tongue: purple. "Those stains will never come off!" he said.

From Catholic school, I knew about stains—the permanent stain of original sin—and I panicked and started bawling. As I blubbered and rubbed my eyes, the tears spread the purple stain across my cheeks. I was convinced that from then on my guilt would be visible on the outside.

Ever since, my taste in pencils has run to the erasable. It was cemented when I was working for Ed Stringham, in the collating department. Ed had a light touch—his handwriting was neat and precise but faint, and that was the problem. The collated proof was sent to the printer by fax, and Ed's markings sometimes did not transmit. Crossing lines was a cardinal sin in collating, so if you wanted to move, say, a whole paragraph on a page that was already a tangle of lines, you had to distinguish that mark somehow, and Ed was in the habit of reaching for the blue pencil. But the fax was colorblind, and, far from standing out, blue did not transmit at all. The men in the makeup department begged Ed not to use blue. He would remember for a while, but soon he would return to his old ways. He was incorrigible.

The men in makeup (they were all men in those days) were pragmatic, and they gave the problem some thought. They knew that they were not going to get rid of Ed. He had been doing this job for some thirty years. Nor were they going to change the handwriting habits of a lifetime by persuading him to bear down more on the pencil. What they could change, though, was the pencil. Joe Carroll, the head of makeup, came back to collating with a couple of boxes of No. 1 pencils, probably purchased from Graham's, the stationery store in the lobby where I had been fitted for my rubber thumb. In the pencil-lead-grading system, No. 1 is a very soft lead, so even if Ed didn't put his back into it, this new pencil would make a darker impression.

My problem was the opposite of Ed's: I bore down on the pencil, and my handwriting was erratic—I'd had complaints about it since third grade—so I often had to erase something and try to neaten it up. The erasures came through on the fax, creating something like a palimpsest. Although I learned a lot in collating, from transcribing the corrections of eminent grammarians, the job of a "scribe" in the medieval sense was probably not ideal for a person who struggled with her handwriting. Mine is a combination of a lot of other people's handwriting:

for a while, I affected the *G* in George Harrison's autograph; I permanently adopted the big top loop and slim descender of a friend's *J*'s. I read somewhere that if you print your *M*'s, making sharp twin peaks of them, it means you hate your mother, and, sure, Mom drove me crazy for much of my life, but I wasn't willing to make that my signature. Somewhere else I read that detached letters showed creativity, and I felt bad that my handwriting betrayed a stodgy flow. The only detachment I had was with the letter *z*, and that was because I'd forgotten how to form a cursive *z*—mine looked like a *y*—and I had to stop and print it. As a teenager, when I entered a contest saying in twenty-five words or less why I deserved to win, say, an eye-makeup kit, or when I wrote a fan letter to Paul McCartney, it was my handwriting as much as my words that I was relying on to charm and captivate. Paul would fall in love with the tail of my racy capital *R*'s. Later, as a graduate student, teaching composition, I noted that the student with the neatest handwriting often wrote the dullest prose.

In the old days at *The New Yorker*, when your pencil point got dull, you just tossed it aside and picked up a new one. There was an office boy who came around in the morning with a tray of freshly sharpened wooden pencils. And they were nice long ones—no stubs. The boy held out his tray of pencils, and you scooped up a quiver of them. It sounds like something out of a dream! Even then I think I knew that the office boy and his tray of pencils would go the way of the ivory-billed woodpecker.

Later, there were boxes and boxes of both No. 1 and No. 2 pencils stacked in the supply closet: all I had to do was grab a box of a dozen, sharpen them up (I used an electric pencil sharpener at the time), and fill my pencil cup. It was downright luxurious.

I spent so many hours dutifully copying changes with a No. 1 pencil that I grew accustomed to the feel of the softer lead. Sometimes an editor, walking around with pencil in hand, would use my desk for a moment to make a change, and leave the pencil behind. It would get mixed in with mine, and if I accidentally took up a pencil that had migrated in this manner, I could feel the difference. I'd take a closer look and, sure enough, there it was embossed on the shaft: No. 2. Writing with a No. 2 pencil made me feel as if I had a hangover. It created a distance between my hand and my brain, put me at a remove from the surface of the paper I was writing on. I would throw it into the desk drawer.

Years later, when I had apparently used up every No. 1 pencil in Times Square, I asked the person in charge of office supplies to order some for me, and she said they weren't available. "What do you mean, they're not available?" I asked. "They're not in the catalogue," she answered. She showed me a thick catalogue of office supplies and told me to choose. I was horrified. The office-supply catalogue reminded me of the catalogue for a vacation club that a friend received when she bought a time-share in Cozumel. She could swap it for any place in the catalogue. But what if the place she wanted to go wasn't in the catalogue? I have always known where I wanted to travel, and always had an overambitious itinerary: London, Canterbury, Dover, Rye, Wye, Swansea, Tintagel, Dublin, Kilkenny, Galway, Mayo, and back to London, with a daytrip to Oxford. Athens, Crete, Rhodes, Cyprus, Samos, Chios, Çanakkale (Troy), Istanbul, Thessaloniki, Skiathos, Delphi, Mycenae, and back to Athens, with a side trip to Sounion to see Byron's graffiti. How could she restrict herself to the places that were in the catalogue?

"Have you ever tried a mechanical pencil?" my colleague

asked. She gave me a mechanical pencil, fixed under rigid plastic to a piece of plasticated cardboard, and a tiny cylinder of replacement lead. I tried—God knows I tried—but I just couldn't do it. I could not master the single click that advances the lead just the right amount (for whom?). I would overclick and the lead would be overlong and it would break. I shook the mechanical pencil, unable to believe that the lead would fall into the right slot without my assistance. I hated having to take it apart to put fresh lead in. I felt as if I were writing with a prosthetic hand. For those of us who like to make marks on paper with graphite mined from the earth, there is no satisfaction in an office-supply catalogue.

Finally, it came to this: I had to buy my own pencils. But it got harder and harder to track down the softest lead. I found a small cache of No. 1 pencils at Rogoff's, a stationery store in Rockaway. Rogoff's is an institution in Rockaway—there is a dentist of the same name. It's the kind of place that a kid looks forward to stopping in on the way to the beach and being allowed to pick out one thing from the aisles and aisles of cheap toys, beach junk, and party goods. The store has a very satisfying stationery aisle, and I feel like a kid in there myself, drooling over the blank books and the party invitations and the different-colored index cards and the pastel legal pads. The shelf with the boxes of pencils was especially alluring, but once I had cleaned out its supply of No. 1s, Rogoff's did not restock.[1]

So one Christmas I went public with my pencil needs: I posted a Wish List online. Items included an iPhone, a Smart Car, hair insurance, a ciborium, and No. 1 pencils. (Small wonder that people were willing to spring for the pencils.) Someone actually

---

1   *Flash: They restocked! I bought two boxes.*

asked, "Are you sure you don't mean No. 2 pencils?" Why would
I make a special plea for something as readily available as a No. 2
pencil? Just the other day I found one lying in the gutter on Park
Avenue South. I picked it up, of course—I may be a prima donna
where pencils are concerned, but you never know when you are
going to be grateful for even a pencil stub. It still astonishes me
that some people claim to prefer No. 2s. They say that, because
the lead is hard, you don't have to sharpen them as often. I say it's
worth the trouble. That December, I received in the mail a full
gross of Dixon Ticonderoga No. 1 pencils as a gift from a secret
admirer. I thought I was set for life.

Thus began years of frustration and abuse. I'd gotten bad
pencils before, but never a whole gross. When I tried to write,
the lead would break; I would sharpen the pencil, and the lead
would break again. As I was sharpening, I could see that the next
segment of lead was not cinched in the wood securely and was
about to break off. I would try to sharpen past it—the way I used
to fast-forward a cassette tape past the part that was mangled—
and discover that the lead was shattered for the entire length of
the pencil. And if it happened with one pencil, it happened with
the whole box.

It was getting embarrassing at the office. I would arrive at
a closing meeting with a handful of pencils and a Magic Rub
eraser. As the points wore down, I would toss them aside; when
the points broke, I felt like an idiot. A writer brandished his
mechanical pencil at me, then opened his suit jacket to reveal a
half-dozen more that he had secreted in his inside breast pocket.
He had a source in the checking department, he explained
devilishly.

I determined to send these pencils back to the dealer. All I knew about them, from the packaging, was that they came from a warehouse in New Jersey. I pictured the pencils being thrown off the truck at a loading dock in the Meadowlands. On the company's Web site I learned that the corporate headquarters of Dixon Ticonderoga was in Florida, and its pencils were made in Mexico. The founder, Joseph Dixon (1799–1869), first opened for business in Salem, Massachusetts. "One of Joseph Dixon's inventions was a heat-resistant graphite crucible widely used in the production of iron and steel during the Mexican-American War. This invention was so successful that Joseph Dixon built a crucible factory in New Jersey, in 1847."

The Web site also provided a little pencil history: "During the 1860's, people still wrote with quill pens and ink, even though Joseph Dixon introduced the first graphite pencil in 1829. It wasn't until the Civil War that the demand for a dry, clean, portable writing instrument became popular and led to the mass production of pencils. Joseph Dixon was the first to develop pencil automation. In 1872, the company was making 86,000 pencils a day."

One of Mr. Dixon's attributes was "an enquiring mind . . . ever alert to seize 'the opportunity offered by the suggestion of the moment.'" This would account for the modern company's various opportunistic lines of pencils, including Ticonderoga Breast Cancer Awareness Pencils, Ticonderoga Pencils with Microban Protection (for writing during flu season?), Ticonderoga EnviroStiks (The Environmentally Friendly Pencil), made from "reforested natural wood." I didn't see any No. 1 pencils. Maybe they had stopped producing them because there was no demand for them anymore.

I summoned the spirit of my mother and of dissatisfied

customers everywhere, and wrote a letter to the CEO of Dixon
Ticonderoga:

> Enclosed find six dozen Dixon Ticonderoga No. 1 pen-
> cils sealed in plastic; seven never-sharpened No. 1s in a box;
> and a dozen used pencils in various stages of breakdown.
> They are what remain of the shipment I received from a
> warehouse in New Jersey in December, 2009. It has been
> very frustrating to deal with these pencils. I couldn't help
> using them, hoping that the next one would not be broken
> inside. I have felt the point bend before breaking and can
> even sense the lead wobbling inside the shaft. Chunks of
> lead have gotten stuck in my electric pencil sharpener at
> work, and I have had to throw the pencil sharpener away.
> Manual sharpeners have had to be disassembled. As part
> of my job, I attend editorial meetings where I act as a kind
> of recording secretary, marking changes in pencil on page
> proofs, and it is not just frustrating but also embarrassing
> when my pencil lead breaks in front of other people.

Mostly, writers of complaining letters are looking for refunds
or free merchandise. I was not sure what I wanted, but it was not
more defective pencils. I had thrown in pencils that had broken in
midsentence. I said I was returning "the unused portion" rather
than putting them in the garbage, because if someone rescued
them, as I had the No. 2 on Park Avenue South, I would be
unleashing on the world the same frustration that the pencils had
caused me. The gist of the letter was, simply, Take these pencils.
Still, I wanted some response, so I probed the reasons for the
poor quality of the pencils:

I would be really curious to know what you think happened. Was the graphite defective? The workmanship? Or was it the shipping that was at fault? Did someone drop them? Where were they made? Do you have quality control? Can you account for the discrepancy between these useless Dixon Ticonderogas and your company's proud history and motto, "The Best of Its Kind"?

———

I didn't have much hope for a response, so I scraped along with four eraserless pencils that I had bought at an art-supply store in the Village. But before long a friend, browsing on pencils.com, discovered that a pencil company called Cal Cedar had brought back the Blackwing—black, with a distinctive flat eraser. Devotees of the Blackwing had been paying up to forty dollars apiece for these pencils after they were discontinued, in 1998. My friend placed an order and gave me a box of twelve Blackwings. The lead is ungraded, but it is definitely softer than a No. 2, and very expressive. The Blackwing motto is "Half the Pressure, Twice the Speed."

I was addicted. They were like Oreos. Soon I was consuming them by the dozen. The descriptions on the boxes are like the tasting notes for wine. The "graphite formulation" of the Palomino Blackwing 602, which is charcoal gray with a black eraser, is "Firm & Smooth." The Palomino Blackwing, black with a white eraser, is "Soft & Smooth." The company has since come out with a white version, called the Blackwing Pearl (I think of it as a First Communion pencil), described as "Balanced & Smooth."

Not long after my first acquisition, Cal Cedar threw a pencil party to celebrate the revival of the Blackwing. The host was Charles Berolzheimer, of Cal Cedar, a sixth-generation pencil-maker. He was dressed in shades of pencil lead. Hundreds of pencil enthusiasts were there, at the Art Directors Club, drawing, graffiti style, on big sheets of white paper, adding to small communal notebooks, creating do-it-yourself thaumatropes, experimenting with the camera obscura and the camera lucida. One woman wore two Blackwings in her hair. A gigantic display pencil hung from the ceiling, and on the way in everyone was given a free pencil, either a Palomino Blackwing or a Palomino Blackwing 602.

A time line of the pencil covered one long wall, documenting the contributions associated with many famous names: Faber, Eberhard, Dixon, da Vinci, Thoreau, Borrowdale (the original graphite lode in England). Among the champions of the Blackwing were Stephen Sondheim, Chuck Jones (the father of Bugs Bunny), John Steinbeck, Vladimir Nabokov, and Faye Dunaway. The time line also included pioneers of such ancillary products as the pencil sharpener and the eraser crimp, but on that night, which was my first foray into the cosmopolitan world of pencils, my favorite fact was this: Every pencil is a sandwich. All these years, I had been wondering how the lead got inside the pencil. It turns out that pencils are made from slats of corrugated wood about the size of a Hershey bar. The graphite is laid in the grooves, another slat is glued on top, and then the sandwich is sawed into individual strips, which are sanded, painted, fitted with ferrules and erasers, and there you have it: delicious Blackwings.

Pencils.com also began to try to tempt me with multicolored erasers, but I was not taken in. The eraser that comes with the Palomino Blackwing is flat, like an elongated Chiclet, fitted into a distinctive flat ferrule by means of a tiny clamp. It can

be extended and slotted back into the ferrule for longer life—
or, better yet, reversed, providing fresh edges for your precision
erasure needs. The flat ferrule keeps the pencil from rolling off
Stephen Sondheim's piano, say.

But I do not rely on the erasers that come crimped into the
tops of pencils. The erasers on my oversupply of defective Dixon
Ticonderogas were virgins. I can always tell that a foreign pencil
has entered my collection when the eraser is worn flat. I make a
lot of mistakes, thus requiring an eraser at least as large as an ice
cube. The eraser available from the catalogue is the Magic Rub,
which is of grayish-white vinyl in the shape of a domino. I use it
to erase the screeds I sometimes feel compelled to write in the
margins of proofs and then regret. Part of my routine is sweep-
ing the eraser crumbs off my desk like foundry dust after every
job. I used to take just one eraser at a time and wear it down to
a nub—a nub that I'd then search for frantically, worried that
the cleaning lady had thrown it out. Now I grab a whole box of
twelve Magic Rubs. When a twelve-pack gets down to the last
layer of three, I get anxious and have to visit the supply cabinet.

As I learned at the pencil party, eraser-tipped pencils have
a contentious history. It was in 1650, in Nuremberg, that lead
was first glued to wood, creating the modern pencil, but it was
not until 1858, according to Henry Petroski's authoritative book
The Pencil, that an enterprising Yank named Hyman Lipman,
of Philadelphia, patented a method of attaching an eraser to the
pencil. Joseph Reckendorfer bought him out and patented a new,
improved eraser-tipped pencil in 1862. In Europe, despite the fact
that in 1864 an eight-foot-long rubber-tipped pencil was carried
in a parade honoring Lothar Faber, the German pencil king, the
eraser is more likely to be sold as a separate item.

In England, erasers are called rubbers, after the material they were originally made from. Actually, that's backwards: rubber got its name because the substance was good for rubbing out mistakes. (What we call rubbers the English call French letters. The French word for eraser is *gomme*.) Before rubber, the material most suited for erasing pencil marks was bread crumbs. A snob might say that the eraser-tipped pencil is like a sofa bed: it sounds like a good idea, but it often features neither the best possible sofa nor the best possible bed. Focusing on the eraser, unscrupulous pencil-makers sometimes stiffed consumers with inferior lead. Or maybe the lead was OK, but the eraser smeared your mistakes around, making them more conspicuous. The effort to combine two distinct things in a single product can result in a decline in the quality of both.

Friends of mine who are artists are particular about erasers; the traces left by an Art Gum or a Pink Pearl—smudges and blurs—can give texture to a drawing. Stick erasers permit artists to erase without laying the meat of their hand on the work. I have seen an eraser made by Koh-i-Noor (a pencil company whose name was meant to evoke precious stones) that was supposed to erase ink and said on its label "imbibed with eraser fluid." There are electric erasers that look like the tool the dental hygienist uses to polish your teeth. A former colleague on the copydesk, the late Bill Walden (stiff-bristle hair, gritted-teeth grin, breast pocket full of writing instruments), had a prototype of a battery-operated eraser; it drilled holes in paper.

According to Petroski, Nabokov remarked that "his pencils outlasted their erasers." (Why didn't Véra give him a Magic Rub?) John Steinbeck "could not use pencils once he felt their ferrules touch his hand." I am in Steinbeck's camp. Once the pencil has reached half its length, that fancy ferrule on the Blackwing digs into my hand. Recently I passed along a whole fistful of used Blackwings to a colleague. I sharpened them first, and she was deeply appreciative. She uses them down to the nub.

At that pencil party, I encountered for the first time a handheld long-point pencil sharpener. Until then, I had not known that a handheld pencil sharpener could be anything but a toy; I have one in the shape of the Empire State Building that I treasure for sentimental reasons, but it is useless except as a cake decoration. The party featured a Sharpening Lounge, where there were state-of-the-art wall-mounted X-Acto sharpeners along one wall (they not only deliver a beautiful point but do so in reverent silence) and copies of a pencil-yellow manual called *How to Sharpen Pencils*, by David Rees. It is one of very few books worthy of the dual category "Humor/Reference."

Until I went to the pencil party, I felt very alone, a crank among co-workers who were content to stick their No. 2 pencils in any of the various electric pencil sharpeners on the premises. And until I read David Rees I hadn't realized why it was that, although I, too, relied on an electric pencil sharpener at work, it left me chronically unsatisfied: you can't see what's going on in there.

David Rees specializes in the artisanal sharpening of No. 2 pencils: for a fee (at first, it was fifteen dollars, but, like everything else, the price of sharpening pencils has gone up), he will hand-sharpen your pencil and return it to you (along with the shavings), its point sheathed in vinyl tubing. "If you can carve a totem pole with a chainsaw then you can sharpen a pencil with a pocketknife," Rees writes. Otherwise, you are better off with an old-fashioned manual pencil sharpener, such as the one that my father mounted on the wall in our basement in Cleveland circa 1960 (Chicago, APSCO Products, with Type 2A Cutter Assembly), or the industrial-strength Boston Ranger 55 that my predecessor Lu Burke gave me, with the warning "It chews pencils." After reading Rees, I took a closer look at Lu's Boston Ranger and found that it has a lever on the crank that you can set for your desired degree of pointedness (B, M, F).

Somewhere along the line, the office boy devolved into an electric pencil sharpener. Mine was a Panasonic, and it gave a pretty good point, if you snatched the pencil out of its jaws in time. But it began to jam more and more frequently, no doubt because I was feeding it from my store of defective No. 1 pencils. I suppose the shattered lead was getting stuck in the blades, but of course I couldn't see in there, much less clean the blades with a soft-bristle toothbrush, as Rees recommends. So I did the next best thing: I unplugged it and beat it against the desk.

One day I received a package in the mail with the return address of a Manny Rodriguez, in Lake Mary, Florida. I had the name mixed up with Manny Ramirez, and wondered what the baseball great was sending me from camp. Inside was a gross of No. 1 pencils and a letter:

Dear Ms. Norris,

Thank you for your letter. I was saddened to see that you had struggled so long with these pencils and I appreciate you taking the time to share the issues you experienced with us. To help bring you some closure to the matter, let me provide some answers for your questions.

Closure! That's what I wanted. Not more pencils but closure. The serious tone of the letter made me wonder: Did I stand in relation to Dixon Ticonderoga as the writers of letters complaining about commas and hyphens stand to me? My first reaction is always along the lines of "Get a life." I am going to try to be more sympathetic to them from now on. I will write back, if only to offer closure.

The letter went on:

Here at Dixon Ticonderoga, we truly do strive to be the best. Each batch of pencils undergoes very stringent quality control measures. We mark all our pencils with a batch code so we can track that batch. When first produced, the batch will undergo various methods of quality control testing which look at everything from the overall appearance of the pencil down to the break strength of the lead. These test results and a sample of each batch is then kept on file for years to come should we have any future issues. Any consumer complaints we receive regarding our pencils are then logged and tracked back to the original batch. We went ahead and pulled the results for batch 219 and can assure you that this batch did pass our quality control methods and that we did not see a complaint history for it.

"Batch 219"—I liked that.

So what happened to your pencils? Your letter very much perked my interest. I personally oversaw the testing [of] your pencils. Although our quality control department and

I have not made it all the way through the seven dozen+ of them, I can say that with many of the sharpened pencils you sent we experienced the same breakage issues. With the pencils from the unopened box, we have not experienced issues with these. As such, we feel there are two possibilities to what went wrong here:

1. Shipping Damage- As you probably know, the number one lead can be a bit fragile. It is extra soft and more susceptible to shipping bumps and bruises. Somewhere along the way before it came to you, these pencils may have been dropped or mishandled in some way. This could cause breakage within the pencil and lead to the issues you have experienced.

2. Sharpener Damage- As pencil sharpeners wear out they can sometimes shatter a pencil's core. Once again, the extra soft lead is more susceptible to this kind of damage. The first time a pencil is sharpened is usually when this occurs. This can be very frustrating as the lead will be shattered after that first instance; however, you will continue to use the pencil and even sharpen it in other sharpeners with the same results, but the damage to the core has already been done. I highly suggest that you replace your sharpener if it is more than a few years old.

It was signed Kristen-Lee Derstein, Marketing Manager, Dixon Ticonderoga Company.

In a very helpful appendix to *How to Sharpen Pencils*, "Pilgrim-age Sites for Pencil Enthusiasts: A Checklist," I learned of the existence of the Paul A. Johnson Pencil Sharpener Museum in Logan, Ohio, in a pocket southeast of Columbus. Ever since wandering into the Sharpening Lounge at the pencil party, I have been keenly aware of the need in this country for a pencil-sharpener boutique. It would be like an Apple store, but more artisanal. Williamsburg would be a good place for it.

Once, passing a storefront in Times Square with the words StubHub in the window, I thought for a moment that my dream had come true . . . but then I remembered that StubHub is a clearinghouse for theater tickets. Given that we still lack a pencil-sharpener boutique, a museum would have to do—maybe it would have a souvenir shop. I knew that Logan also had a canoe livery and a washboard factory, and I pictured myself, in Thoreau mode, paddling from the washboard factory to the pencil-sharpener museum, ideally in the company of David Rees. Rees himself had never visited the Chartres of pencil-sharpener pilgrimages, and unfortunately was not free to join me. He had done his research, however, and warned me that the collection consisted mainly of novelty pencil sharpeners.

So on a perfect late-summer day, I went by myself, making a substantial detour on the way back to New York from the annual weekend on Kelleys Island, in Lake Erie. Leaving the island, I took the ferry to Marblehead, at the tip of the peninsula that forms Sandusky Bay, and instead of swinging east through Cleve-land, as usual, I headed south: Route 4 to Bucyrus, 98 to Waldo, 23 to Columbus, which I skirted on I-270, and 33 past Lancaster to Logan. The air was pungent with fertilizer. There were acres of corn and pumpkins, the landscape bisected arbitrarily by train tracks. I was dazzled by a sign for SIAM: maybe it was the effect of all that corn, but it looked like MAIS spelled backwards. On entering Chatfield, I was gratified by a typo on a reader board: "Chatfield Canvas & Upholstrey." Outside Delaware, Ohio, there was a cemetery advertising "½ Price Graves." I passed a turnoff for Gender Road. Maybe it was named for a guy name Gender, or maybe it was the road to a theme park where everything was masculine, feminine, or neuter.

The Paul A. Johnson Pencil Sharpener Museum is at the Hocking Hills Welcome Center. The museum is a freestanding prefab cabin decorated with a clutch of oversized colored pencils. Admission is free. I entered reverently. A plaque at the entrance commemorates the Reverend Johnson (1925–2010), and framed newspaper clippings document the collection, of more than 3,400 pencil sharpeners, and its move from Carbon Hill, in nearby Nelsonville, to the welcome center, where it officially reopened in 2011. Johnson started the collection after he retired from the ministry, in 1988. His wife, Charlotte, knowing he would need something to occupy him in retirement, gave him two pencil sharpeners in the shape of metal cars for Christmas. He spent the next eleven years searching "for unique designs and models." One of his principal sources of pencil sharpeners was hospital gift shops.

Rees would approve of one of the rules governing Johnson's acquisitions: the museum accepts no electric pencil sharpeners. (Johnson made an exception for a gorilla that one of his grandchildren gave him; its eyes glow red when the pencil is sharpened.) Johnson never used his pencil sharpeners. When asked why he collected them, he said, "Nobody else does it."

The sharpeners are arrayed behind glass, on glass shelves, according to category: Transportation, Music (harp, gramophone, banjo, accordion, organ), Military, Space, History (the Colosseum, the Empire State Building—that's the one I have!—the Golden Gate Bridge, Christ the Redeemer with arms outspread on that mountaintop in Rio), the Zodiac, Dogs, Cats, Christmas, Easter (what, no Passover sharpeners?), Hearts, Sports, Furniture/Household (bathtub, electric fan, sewing machine, cash register), and so on. There were a few technical categories, including dual-hole sharpeners (some in the shape of noses—ouch) and sharpeners for flat pencils, the kind carpenters use. I took as many pictures as I could. Only a sign warning that the museum is under surveillance twenty-four hours a day kept me from dancing.

Inside the welcome center, I examined a copy of the patent for the oldest sharpener in the collection and a small selection of sharpeners arrayed around it on the wall: a toilet, a submarine, a trumpet, a caboose. A beautiful cardinal's head (a bird's, not the prelate's) made me wonder whether there was a series of ornithological pencil sharpeners and whether the Vatican carried an ecclesiastical line.

I spoke with Karen Raymore, a blond woman wearing black dotted swiss, who had come to Ohio from Wisconsin, where she was in destination marketing. It was she who had put the pencil-sharpener museum on the map. Driving out toward Nelsonville one day, she had spotted the sign that the Reverend Johnson had posted, inviting passersby to visit the pencil-sharpener museum—at the time, it was set up on his property, in Carbon Hill—and providing a phone number. She had arranged a tour for a group of travel writers. When Raymore heard that the Reverend Johnson had died, she worried: "What are they going to do with that collection?" She had known a couple who had a lunch-box museum. It was attached to their diner. If you told the man what kind of lunch box you had had as a child, he could tell you the year you were born. (I had a classic red plaid in first grade. Later, when we moved to the land of Blanks and Dashes, I had an Augie Doggie, which I regretted.) When the lunch-box connoisseur died, his widow could not cope, so she closed the diner, and the lunch-box museum was lost. Raymore was determined that the pencil-sharpener museum would not go the same way.

"It just so happened that the family didn't know what to do with the museum," she said, and they were happy to entrust it to the Hocking Hills Tourism Association. Susie McKinnon, the curator of the pencil-sharpener museum, photographed the exact setup, with the pencil sharpeners arranged in categories on open shelves, and wrapped each sharpener individually. Meanwhile, the welcome center prepared a foundation and moved the prefab building onto it. When the museum reopened, in the summer of 2011, "it just so happened that it was a slow news day," Raymore went on, "and one hundred and thirty-two news outlets from around the world"—everywhere from Australia to Saudi Arabia—"picked up the story. So we had our fifteen seconds of fame."

Fifty thousand people a year stop at the Hocking Hills Welcome Center. Perhaps not all of them take the opportunity to examine the pencil-sharpener collection, but certainly far more people see it now than when it was off a road in Carbon Hill. The Reverend Johnson's daughter told Raymore, "Dad always said he hoped it would end up here."

Susie McKinnon told me that there were 3,441 pencil sharpeners in the museum. The Reverend Johnson had a rule:

each pencil sharpener had to be unique—no duplicates. McKinnon elaborated on Johnson's definition of "unique": it could mean that a sharpener was the same shape but a different color, or highly polished instead of dull. He would buy a package of a dozen to acquire one in a color he didn't have, and give the rest away as gifts. I had noticed a series of bears straddling tree trunks marked variously "Drive-Thru Tree Park" and "California Redwoods." The museum does accept contributions to the collection—if someone has what she thinks is a unique piece, she can e-mail McKinnon a photograph. Having taken pictures of the exhibit in situ and handled each pencil sharpener before moving the collection, McKinnon can tell right away whether a sharpener fits the unique qualification. She herself donated a wooden sharpener in the shape of a cat playing with a ball of yarn. A woman who was moving sent photos of fifty pencil sharpeners, which led to forty-eight new acquisitions. A year earlier, McKinnon had heard from a man in the Virgin Islands who was wondering whether the museum would be interested in a ten-pound cast-iron sharpener that had belonged to his father, who had died recently, at the age of eighty-four. She had not heard back from him, but had reason to hope for the bequest. "It would date to about 1904," she said. "That would not make it the oldest in the collection but the largest of the oldest." The oldest include some tiny clip-ons from the early 1900s, presumably for the nerd ancestors of men who keep pens in their shirt pockets, as well as one ancient sharpener still in its own leather pouch, and another in the shape of a diminutive, elegantly dressed lady. I had noticed these, on a shelf in a corner labeled Special. I asked, hopefully, "Is a catalogue in the works?"

"No, it is not," McKinnon said decisively.

McKinnon asked me not to advertise the fact, but that sign

saying that the museum is under twenty-four-hour surveillance came with the house. There is not a lot of pencil-sharpener-related crime in the Hocking Hills.

While we were talking, I had an idea. I was traveling with a black KUM long-point sharpener, and I didn't see anything like it in the collection. It was the handheld model I had seen at the pencil party; I had ordered so many pencils that Cal Cedar threw in a free sharpener. I loved having it with me, to sharpen pencils on the go or to whip out in a café if a friend's point had gotten dull. The collection included some double-hole sharpeners, and McKinnon had assumed, as many people do, that one hole was for regular pencils and the other for colored pencils. I explained how it worked: the cylinders beneath the blades are angled differently, and each pencil goes first in one hole, for whittling away the wood, and then in the other, for grinding the graphite. McKinnon seemed genuinely interested, though I did not test her interest by going into detail about the way I like to keep the lid up while I'm in the wood hole, so that the shaving can unfurl all in one piece. It's a little like trying to peel an apple in one continuous strip: the shaving comes out in a paper-thin spiral, and the hexagonal shape of the pencil produces a pinking-shear effect edged with the color of the pencil shaft, a satisfying deep gray in the case of the Blackwing 602. It looks like a tiny tiered skirt for a toothpick doll. I have had people, even fellow pencil fanciers, back away from me when I describe this, although they might be tempted to do it themselves, in private. I perch the intact spirals on the shelf and there they remain, until some puzzled cleaning lady throws them away.

I went back to my car, found the pencil sharpener just where I had packed it, in a pocket of the zippered compartment on my backpack, and photographed it on the back of my car before shaking out the shavings in the parking lot. I did not want the fact that my sharpener was not a virgin to make it ineligible for display in the museum.

"I can tell you right now that we don't have this," McKinnon said. I was thrilled. I felt as if I were a part of southern Ohio pencil history. She grabbed her keys, and we went back out to the museum. "Where will it fit?" I said. The sharpeners were crowded into their arrangements on the shelves. McKinnon decided that it belonged with the other two-hole sharpeners (but not the noses). She unlocked the door and swung it open, shoved the museum pieces together a little, and gave my black Palomino Blackwing long-point a prominent position at the front of the case. I was hoping she'd open some more of the glass doors so that I could take pictures without the glare, but my mission was accomplished at the Paul A. Johnson Pencil Sharpener Museum, so I let Susie go back to her office and I hit the road.

THE MILLION-DOLLAR
COPY EDITOR

T HE WORDS "MILLIONAIRE" AND "COPY EDITOR" hardly
ever land in the same sentence, much less describe the same
person, but Lu Burke was that rare thing: a copy editor who
became a millionaire. She worked at *The New Yorker* from 1958
to 1990, when she retired to Southbury, Connecticut, and a
year after she died, in October 2010, reportedly of leukemia, it
emerged that Lu had willed her entire estate, of more than a million dollars, to the Southbury Public Library. I used to stop and
see her once in a while on my way to Massachusetts, and we'd
have lunch at Friendly's, but with Lu hungry for gossip about
the old crew, a visit could turn a three-and-half-hour drive into a
daylong journey. By the time she died, I hadn't seen her in years,
and I felt bad about that, so finding out that Lu had been sitting
on a million dollars made me feel a little better.

Lu had always been protective of her privacy, so skilled at

deflecting any personal questions that it was not until her will was probated, and a writer for *Connecticut Magazine* started calling up and asking questions, that we realized we didn't know the first thing about her. We knew she liked Trollope and loved jazz. She lived on Horatio Street, in Greenwich Village. She once dated J. D. Salinger. Back in the sixties, she had written letters to the *Village Voice*, tangling with Norman Mailer. On one occasion, she told a co-worker that the happiest time of her life was the summer she spent at a camp where she was issued a bugle and blew reveille every morning. But we didn't know where she was from, or where she had gone to school, or what her real first name was—Lu had to be short for something.

At Pomperaug Woods, an assisted-living center in Southbury that she moved into from the retirement community of Heritage Village, Lu disdained to join the other residents in the dining room, preferring to carry her meals up to her apartment and dine alone. A story that made the rounds after her death was that once, while waiting for the elevator, she beckoned to a fellow resident and asked, "Would you do me a favor?" And when the woman said yes, Lu told her, "Drop dead."

———

Lu Burke is now the immortal patron of the Southbury Public Library. I felt a little sheepish making a special trip to the library when I had not gone out of my way to visit Southbury while Lu was alive, but I was curious. The library's address, 100 Poverty Road, is not indicative of its condition. The sign at the foot of the driveway says "Since 1776," meaning that the town of Southbury has had some kind of library, and employed a librarian, ever since colonial days, but the new Southbury Public Library, with Palladian windows, a portico, and a railed roof deck, on six acres that used to be a pumpkin patch, opened in 2006. It did not even smell like a library yet. It was easy to see that Lu would have thought this was a good repository for her hard-earned cash, but also difficult to see what more was needed. All the appointments were in exquisite taste—there were Bill Blass reading lamps in the reference section, leather club chairs and a gas fireplace in a reading room, lots of large-print books and jigsaw puzzles for the geezers, a children's library with two suits of armor, a dozen computers, free Wi-Fi, Kindles to borrow, a terrace, one of those stands that dispense plastic bags for wet umbrellas, and the ultimate luxury for a book lover: shelves that were still empty.

When the gift was announced, the library's board, made up of nine volunteers appointed by the selectmen, began searching for appropriate ways to honor Lu's intent. "We are great strategic planners," Shirley Michaels, the head of the library board, told me. "Just to spend money frivolously is not our idea." They decided to name the circulation desk for Lu—a magnificent thirty-four-foot-long dark-cherrywood installation that would not have been out of place in a cathedral—and to inaugurate a literary program, which they planned to kick off in May, with a *New Yorker* Fiction Night. It was canceled, however, and the order for the granite plaque was put on hold, when Southbury's newly elected first selectman, Ed Edelson, no doubt attracted by the size of Lu's gift, decided to look into the financial arrangement between the town and the library. He found that the town owns the library—

not the other way around—and that the library's funds, which, including Lu's bequest, would amount to $1.8 million, belonged in a town account. He said on the phone, "To have town accounts managed by volunteers seems to me not to be the appropriate way to go." The board was insulted. "For fifty years, we've never had a first selectman try to grab the money," Michaels said.

Edelson said he was impressed by two things: Lu Burke's generosity (actually, Lu was not known for that trait; a copy editor does not accrue a million dollars through generosity) and the fact that she hadn't been involved in the library. As far as anyone knew, she never even had a library card. Nobody at the library knew who she was, so how could they know what she would have wanted them to spend her money on? Edelson went to the probate office and found out that Lu Burke had left the money for the "general purposes of the library." His first idea was "Well, can we use the money to buy books?" He proposed that the town stop using taxpayers' money to buy books—the town has budgeted fifty thousand dollars annually for library books—and use Lu Burke's money instead, spending down the bequest over twenty years. The response to that was "No way." "It would be as if it never happened," Michaels said.

The press surrounding Lu's bequest flushed out her next of kin. Stephanie Blansett, who worked as a school-nurse supervisor in Nashville, Tennessee, left a comment in response to an article about Lu in an online news outlet called the Southbury Patch. She identified herself as Lu Burke's niece. Her father, John Seiter, was Lu's half brother; he was nine years older than Lu. Stephanie divulged, shockingly, that Lu's given name was Lulu. "Lu never was a Lulu," Stephanie said, when I reached her by phone.

Edelson finally relented, allowing the library and its supporters to spend Lu's money as they wished. A celebration of the bequest was held on May 22, 2013. I went up to Southbury again, this time with Alice Quinn, the former poetry editor of *The New Yorker*, who filled me in on the resolution of the dispute. There would be no "draw down," the selectman's idea of using Lu's money instead of the taxpayers' to cover the annual book budget. The library would keep the money as discretionary funds, to be rolled over from year to year, and the town will continue to support the library despite the library's being loaded.

The spacious parking lot was not quite full on this fine night, and the umbrella bagger was not in demand. It was the kind of amenity that I couldn't quite picture Lu paying for (and she hadn't; the Friends of the Library buys furnishings with proceeds from its yearly book sale). Catering was courtesy of the Naugatuck Savings Bank: a tasteful selection of appetizers, wine, dessert, and coffee. The tone was festive without being bubbly.

Shirley Michaels and Shirley Thorson, the head librarian, greeted us. I lurked on the fringes of a group where Ed Edelson was holding forth, at a high cocktail table strewn with party favors (ballpoint pens from the Naugatuck Savings Bank). When Michaels ascended the stairs to begin the formal proceedings, I ducked over to stand with Alice at the foot of the stairs and unobtrusively retrieved from my bag the prop I had brought along: Lu's comma shaker, a relic dating approximately to the early 1960s.

The big moment was the unveiling of the plaque for the Lu Burke Circulation Desk. Alice had brought along a *Webster's Second Unabridged* to donate to the library in honor of Lu, and there was a stand on the desk waiting to receive it. The dictionary opened to the page with "Life" as the guide word in the upper right-hand corner.

Michaels introduced Alice as Lu Burke's colleague. Alice explained that her father had lived in Pomperaug Woods, and she recognized Lu there when she went to visit him. Neither Lu nor Alice was sure of the other's identity at first, but the next time Alice visited she approached. Lu said, "So you've materialized." I could hear Lu's voice in that choice of words.

Then Alice introduced me. I had not prepared any formal remarks. While waiting on West Forty-third Street for Alice to pick me up in her Prius (the hybrid, which runs quietly and burns fuel efficiently, seemed like the perfect car for a poetry editor), I'd scribbled a few things down. We really do think of Lu every day at the office. I would have liked to ask her opinion about a spelling conundrum we had had that week at the office: whether or not to double the *t* in the past tense of the verb "to summit," as in "Traditionally, the Sherpas summitted Everest each season before the Western clients on guided tours." The Little Red Web does actually include this sense of "summit" as an intransitive verb ("to climb to the summit"), but I didn't see it, possibly because I was thrown by the first sense: "to participate in a summit conference." Our rule is to double the consonant if the dictionary offers it as an alternative. How could we assume it would be an alternative if we didn't see it in the dictionary at all?

I knew this stuff wasn't going to fly. I wanted to conjure Lu's spirit somehow. I used to have to give myself little pep talks in order not to be afraid of Lu. She had made me cry on my first day in collating, when I not only could not find what she wanted but had no idea what she was talking about. I would tell myself that

I hadn't done anything wrong, and so I had nothing to fear. And if you kept standing up to Lu, eventually you won her respect. I also learned from her example not to be like her. I hope.

Then I held up the comma shaker. Although it was right there in my hand for everyone to see, I had to describe it, because the hand-drawn commas on it have faded over the years, and it was an object of some subtlety to begin with. I demonstrated its use by giving the air a generous sprinkling of commas. Then I embarked on a reminiscence about how the copydesk used to be near the elevator vestibule where Mr. Shawn would meet Lillian Ross and her dog Goldie when they left at night. I omitted everything about the relationship between Mr. Shawn and Miss Ross (she was his girlfriend), and the breed of the dog (an apricot poodle). I also left out the part about the time Goldie peed in the hall and I mopped it up. Mr. Shawn was grateful for my swift application of the paper towel. I imagined he admired my genetic predisposition to spring into the role of cleaning lady. He himself was, of course, unable to cope with the situation or stand by holding the leash while Miss Ross did the wiping up. I had a pretty shrewd idea that Mr. Shawn would have to accept my next "letter from a friend."

One afternoon when Miss Ross was waiting for Mr. Shawn at the bottom of the stairs that led up to the twentieth floor, Goldie started barking. It was an absurd sound to hear in the halls of America's premier literary magazine, and when the trio left, Lu came out of her office and stood in the hall. *"Arf, arf!"* she said, in imitation of Goldie. *"Arf, arf, arf!"*

Suddenly my remarks were over. I could not top Lu's mischievous imitation of Goldie barking in the hall. Shirley Michaels had said that everyone was curious about the library's mysterious benefactor, so I said that anyone who had a question about Lu should feel free to ask Alice or me. Just then, a little censor kicked in at the back of my brain. Was the "me" correct? Yes: it was the indirect object of "ask." Lu would have cringed if I had committed the sin of overcorrectness and said to "ask Alice or I." There was nothing vulgar about using the pronoun "me." It was definitely "ask Alice or me."

ACKNOWLEDGMENTS

The seeds of this book were broadcast by John Bennet, of *The New Yorker*, who encouraged me to write something—anything. Eleanor Martin and Sasha Weiss were more selective, and Michael Agger was ready to get his hands dirty. David Remnick's approval was like sunshine. Vicky Raab introduced me to Andy Ross and Leigh Haber, and Emily Nunn recommended me to David Kuhn, who, with Becky Sweren, developed the proposal that attracted Matt Weiland, at W. W. Norton, who pruned my wild prose into something resembling a topiary garden.

I am grateful to James Salter for allowing me to quote from our correspondence on commas and to Nick Paumgarten for putting us in touch. And I am indebted to all the *New Yorker* writers whose prose I've had the pleasure of working on over the years, and especially to John McPhee, George Saunders, Ian Frazier, Mark Singer, Emily Nussbaum, Jon Lee Anderson, Lauren Collins, Kelefa Sanneh, Calvin Trillin, Karen Russell, and Ben McGrath, whose work I've taken the liberty of quoting, as well as to Charles McGrath, an editor and a gentleman, and to Alice Russell-Shapiro, one intrepid *New Yorker* reader.

A project like this necessarily draws on many co-conspirators, witting and un-. For support both personal and professional I am indebted to Ann Goldstein, Nancy Holyoke, and Elizabeth Pearson-Griffiths. For asking pesky questions and insisting that she valued my impatient answers, Carol Anderson. For not asking questions, Andrew Boynton. For classics, Charles Mercier. For lexicography, Peter Sokolowski. For hyphens, John M. Morse. For big words, Jeffrey Gustavson. For dirty words, Nick Trautwein. For Emily Dickinson scholarship, Sharon Cameron. For insights into Japanese, Lindsley Miyoshi and Susan Fischer. For Basque, Elizabeth Macklin. For dashes, Jeffrey Frank. For background on Eleanor Gould and Lu Burke, Susan Packard and Stephanie Seiter Blansett. For the "flower," Janet Malcolm. For jousting with Lu Burke, Becky Sawyer. For popping up unexpectedly, Alice Quinn. For custody of the comma shaker, Julie Just. For determination, Shirley Michaels, of the Southbury Public Library. For generosity and good will, Sean Wilsey. For taking an interest for no good reason, Philip Hoare. For her stabs at who and whom, Little Annie Bandez. For her fidelity to the subjective case, Diane Englander. For fellowship among the apostrophes and the semicolons, Penelope Rowlands. For her artist's eye, Toby Schust Allan. For solidarity in pencils and pencil sharpeners, Nancy Franklin, Blake Eskin, Michael Specter, and David Rees; in Ohio, Karen Raymore and Susie McKinnon; and Kristen-Lee Derstein at Dixon Ticonderoga. For peace and quiet, Gregory Maguire, in Vermont; J. Kathleen White, in the East Village; Mary J. Martin Schaefer, in Provincetown; and the Provincetown Public Library. And for sharing my good fortune with such zest and humor, Paula and Nathan Rothstein, Roni Gross, Peter Schell, Cynthia Cotts, Alice Truax, Yevgenia Margolis, Janet Abramowicz, Susan Miller, and Victoria Roberts. Also Bruce Diones, Rebecca Mead, Pat Keogh, Rhonda Sherman, Brenda Phipps, Henry Finder, and Daniel Zalewski. For late saves, Betsy Morais and Emily Greenhouse. For technical assistance, Sam MacLaughlin, at Norton; Pat Coll, who chased down the permissions; Otto Sonntag, who dared to copy-edit the copy editor; and Don Rifkin, who double-dared. For promotional efforts, Erin Lovett.

And I am indebted for sustenance to my faithful friends and fellow-writers Susan Grimm, Mary Grimm, Kristin Ohlson, Tricia Springstubb, Mary Louise Robison (R.I.P.), Charles Oberndorf, Susan Carpenter, Donna Jarrell, Jeff Gundy, Tom Bishop, and the Kelleys Island Regulars, as well as to the late Mary Beth Richlovsky. Clancey O'Connor and Denise Rodino have given me unconditional love. Richard H. Smith and Barrett J. Mandel were teachers of lasting influence, and Garret Keizer, a fellow student, has taught by example. I would not be who I am if it were not for my parents, Miles and Eileen Norris; my wonderful brother Miles and my fabulous sister Baby Dee; my grandmother Mary B. Norris; and my fairy godparents, Peter F. Fleischmann and Jeanne Cowles Wilson Fleischmann Bruce.

NOTES

ix **"Of course, when you correct"**: Francis A. Burkle-Young and Saundra Rose Maley, *The Art of the Footnote: The Intelligent Student's Guide to the Art and Science of Annotating Texts* (Lanham, MD: University Press of America, 1996), p. 81.

Introduction: Confession of a Comma Queen

7 **"In the view's right-middle ground"**: John McPhee, "Coming into the Country—IV," *The New Yorker*, July 11, 1977, p. 38. This and McPhee's other pieces about Alaska were later collected as *Coming into the Country* (New York: Farrar, Straus and Giroux, 1978).

8 **It's from the Greek**: *Merriam-Webster's Collegiate Dictionary*, 11th ed., s.v. "synecdoche."

Chapter 1: Spelling Is for Weirdos

18 **"Several of our vowels"**: Noah Webster, *A Grammatical Institute, of the English Language*, 1st ed. (Hartford, CT: Hudson & Goodwin [1783]), p. 5. Facsimile edition printed at Paladin Commercial

Printers for the Noah Webster House, Inc., and Museum of West Hartford History, West Hartford, CT.

20 **"the forgotten founding father"**: Joshua Kendall, *The Forgotten Founding Father: Noah Webster's Obsession and the Creation of an American Culture* (New York; G. P. Putnam's Sons, 2010).

21 **"born definer"**: Ibid., p. 5.

22 **"Spelling is the art"**: Webster, *Grammatical Institute*, p. 24.

23 **"These words are vulgarly"**: Ibid., p. 33 (note).

26 **"Americans rejected *ake*"**: Harlow Giles Unger, *Noah Webster: The Life and Times of an American Patriot* (New York: John Wiley and Sons, 1998), p. 252.

Chapter 2: That Witch!

51 **"But rock columns are"**: John McPhee, "Annals of the Former World: In Suspect Terrain—II," *The New Yorker*, Sept. 20, 1982, p. 47. This and other pieces about the geology of North America were collected in *In Suspect Terrain* (New York: Farrar, Straus and Giroux, 1983), which was in turn collected in *Annals of the Former World* (New York: Farrar, Straus and Giroux, 1998).

52 **"As we drank tea"**: Lauren Collins, "Sark Spring," *The New Yorker*, Oct. 29, 2012, p. 55.

53 **"Walking down the long"**: Edward St. Aubyn, *Mother's Milk*, in *The Patrick Melrose Novels* (New York: Picador, 2012), p. 496.

54 **"While picking kids up at school"**: George Saunders, "The Semplica-Girl Diaries," *The New Yorker*, Oct. 15, 2012, p. 69. This story was later collected in *Tenth of December* (New York: Random House, 2013).

Chapter 3: The Problem of Heesh

59 **"the words male and female"**: David Marsh, *For Who the Bell Tolls: One Man's Quest for Grammatical Perfection* (London: Guardian Faber Publishing, 2013), p. 232.

60 **"English . . . has certain unusual"**: Robert Graves and Alan

Hodge, *The Reader Over Your Shoulder*, (New York: Vintage Books, 1979), pp. 6–7.

60 **"Gender is illogical"**: Ibid., p. 7.

62 **"a poor little weak thing"**: Mark Twain, "The Awful German Language." See http://www.crossmyt.com/hc/linghebr/awfgrmlg.html.

63 **"Every noun has a gender"**: Ibid.

63 **"She fit him totally"**: American Masters: *LENNONYC*, a documentary; premiered on PBS December 4, 2012; aired again on March 21, 2014; Michael Epstein, director/writer. See http://video.pbs.org/video/2309422687/; http://www.pbs.org/wnet/americanmasters/episodes/lennonyc/about-the-film/1551/.

64 **"English has a number"**: Bryan A. Garner, *Garner's Modern American Usage*, 3rd ed. (New York: Oxford University Press, 2009), p. 739.

64 **"If the English language had"**: Milne, quoted in Marsh, *For Who the Bell Tolls*, p. 225.

65 **Alternatives come from all over**: These examples are from Dennis Baron, "The Epicene Pronouns: A Chronology of the Word That Failed." See http://www.english.illinois.edu/-people-/faculty/debaron/essays/epicene.htm. Earlier versions of this list appeared in "The Epicene Pronoun: The Word That Failed," *American Speech* 56 (1981): 83–97; and *Grammar and Gender* (New Haven and London: Yale University Press, 1986).

66 **"spontaneously appeared in Baltimore"**: See Elaine M. Stotko and Margaret Troyer, "A New Gender-Neutral Pronoun in Baltimore, Maryland: A Preliminary Study," *American Speech* 82, no. 3 (2007): 262–79.

66 **"that refer . . . to antecedents"**: C. Marshall Thatcher, "What Is 'EET'? A Proposal to Add a Series of Referent-Inclusive Third Person Singular Pronouns and Possessive Adjectives to the English Language for Use in Legal Drafting," *South Dakota Law Review* 59, no. 1 (2014): 79–89. "What Is Eet?" is viewable online at http://works.bepress.com/cgi/viewcontent.cgi?article=1011&context=charles_thatcher.

66 **"To talk of *persons*"**: H. W. Fowler, *A Dictionary of Modern English*

Usage, 2nd ed., revised by Sir Ernest Gowers (New York: Oxford University Press, 1965), p. 221.

67 **"where the matter of sex"**: Ibid., p. 404 (entry for "number," 11).

68 **"The aspirant can then sink"**: Dwight Garner, "Creative Writing, via a Workshop or the Big City," *New York Times*, Feb. 26, 2014.

68 **"the horrible *their*"**: Fowler, *Dictionary of Modern English Usage*, p. 417.

68 **"Though the masculine singular"**: Garner, *Garner's Modern American Usage*, p. 740.

69 **"If they can do it"**: Marsh, *For Who the Bell Tolls*, p. 230.

69 **" 'A person can't help their birth' "**: William Makepeace Thackeray, *Vanity Fair* (1847–48; reprint, New York: Penguin Classics, 2001), p .483.

70 **"Such phrases are often alternated"**: Garner, *Garner's Modern American Usage*, p. 739 (entry for "Sexism," B. The Pronoun Problem).

71 **"the method carries two risks"**: Ibid., p. 739–40.

Chapter 4: Between You and Me

78 **"any exact notion of what is taking place"**: E. B. White, from the introduction to "Will Strunk" in *Essays of E. B. White* (New York: HarperPerennial, 1999), p. 319.

79 **David Foster Wallace lists**: David Foster Wallace, "Tense Present: Democracy, English, and the Wars over Usage," *Harper's*, April 2001, p. 39. Later collected as "Authority and American Usage" in *Consider the Lobster and Other Essays* (Boston: Little, Brown, 2005).

82 **"The King and I"**: Example from Ben Yagoda, *How to Not Write Bad* (New York: Riverhead Books, 2013), p. 99.

87 **"verbs of the senses"**: Karen Elizabeth Gordon, *The Transitive Vampire* (New York: Times Books, 1984), p. 29.

88 **"The *who/whom* distinction"**: Steven Pinker, *The Language Instinct* (New York: William Morrow, 1994), p. 116.

89 **"the dissident blogger, whom"**: Jon Lee Anderson, "Private Eyes," *The New Yorker*, Oct. 21, 2013, p. 71.

90 **"If someone approaches"**: Randy Steel, "9 Things NOT to Do After a Breakdown," AAA New York, *C&T* 3, no. 3 (March 2014): 37.

Chapter 5: Comma Comma Comma Comma, Chameleon

94   **The editors of *Webster's Third***: David Skinner, *The Story of Ain't: America, Its Language, and the Most Controversial Dictionary Ever Published* (New York: Harper, 2012), p. 281.

96   **"But what principally attracted"**: Charles Dickens, *The Life and Adventures of Nicholas Nickleby* (1839; reprint, New York: Oxford University Press, 1982), pp. 448, 449.

96   **"The first house to which"**: Ibid., p. 310.

97   **"She brought *me*"**: *The Selected Letters of Charles Dickens*, edited by Jenny Hartley (New York: Oxford University Press, 2012), p. 311.

97   **"Often I have lain thus"**: Herman Melville, *White-Jacket* (1850; reprint, Evanston: Northwestern University Press, 1970), p. 119.

101 **"Before Atwater died"**: The line is from Jane Mayer, "Attack Dog," *The New Yorker*, Feb. 13 and 20, 2012, cited in Ben Yagoda, "Fanfare for the Comma Man," *New York Times*, April 9, 2012.

103 **"When I was in high school"**: Marc Fisher, "The Master," *The New Yorker*, April 1, 2013, p. 38.

104 **"Eve was across the room"**: James Salter, *Light Years* (New York: Vintage, 1995), p. 27.

106 **"She smiled that stunning, wide smile"**: Ibid., p. 181.

107 **"It was as if they were"**: Ibid., p. 231.

107 **"The ship was enormous"**: Ibid., p. 263.

107 **"He sailed on the *France*"**: Ibid., p. 262.

109 **"Is there anything in your"**: Jennifer Schuessler, "A Proper Celebration of the Not-So-Proper Modern British Novel," *New York Times*, July 24, 2013.

Chapter 6: Who Put the Hyphen in *Moby-Dick*?

118 **"How was it?"**: Karen Russell, "The Bad Graft," *The New Yorker*, June 9 and 16, 2014, pp. 97–98.

119 **"My father specialized"**: Edward N. Teall, *Meet Mr. Hyphen (And Put Him in His Place)* (New York: Funk & Wagnalls, 1937), p. 31.

119 **footnote on "po-lop-o-ny"**: Ibid., p. 19.

119 **"It should be regarded"**: Ibid., p. 14.

120 **"Nothing is to be gained"**: Ibid., p. 57.

120 **"Did you ever see a hyphen"**: Ibid., p. 77.

121 **"an excess of academic affectation"**: Ibid., p. 90.

124 **"Oh, Time, Strength, Cash"**: Herman Melville, *Moby-Dick* (1851; reprint, New York: Modern Library, 1992), p. 207.

125 **posted online with artwork**: See http://www.mobydickbigread.com.

125 **"And the women of New Bedford"**: Melville, *Moby-Dick*, p. 47.

129 **"It is thought here"**: The letter is described in Andrew Delbanco, *Melville: His World and Work* (New York: Vintage Books, 2006), p. 177.

129 **"The proofs . . . were replete"**: Herman Melville, *Pierre*, cited in Delbanco, *Melville*, pp. 177–78.

129 **"Commas were sometimes used"**: G. Thomas Tanselle, in *Typee, Omoo, Mardi*, by Herman Melville (New York: Library of America, 1982), pp. 1324–25.

130 **"In his letter Allan spells"**: G. Thomas Tanselle, in *Redburn, White-Jacket, Moby-Dick*, by Herman Melville (New York: Library of America, 1983).

Chapter 7: A Dash, a Semicolon, and a Colon Walk into a Bar

137 **"I know how you must feel"**: Jeffrey Frank, *Ike and Dick: Portrait of a Strange Political Marriage* (New York: Simon and Schuster, 2013), pp. 253–54.

138 **"In Dickinson's poetry"**: Cristanne Miller, *Emily Dickinson: A Poet's Grammar* (Cambridge: Harvard University Press, 1987), p. 53.

138 **she "relied mainly on dashes"**: R. W. Franklin, ed., *The Poems of Emily Dickinson* (Cambridge: Harvard University Press, 2005), p. 10.

138 **book review by Judith Thurman**: "A New Reading of Emily Dickinson," *The New Yorker*, Aug. 3, 2008, pp. 68–73.

139 **Today, the entire archive**: See www.edickinson.org.

142 **"You must wait—you"**: *The Aspern Papers*, in *The Henry James Reader*, ed. Leon Edel (New York: Scribner, 1965), p. 235.

143 **"She *was* bad; but"**: Henry James, *Washington Square*, in Edel, ed., *The Henry James Reader*, p. 89.

143 **"Poor Catherine was conscious"**: Ibid.

144 **"You have taken up"**: Ibid., pp. 86–87.

145 **"Unable to visit Bruichladdich"**: Kelefa Sanneh, "Spirit Guide," *The New Yorker*, Feb. 11 and 18, 2013, p. 51.

146 **Baker calls "dashtards"**: Nicholson Baker, "The History of Punctuation," in *The Size of Thoughts: Essays and Other Lumber* (New York: Random House, 1996), quoted by Keith Houston in *Shady Characters: The Secret Life of Punctuation, Symbols, and Other Typographical Marks* (New York: W. W. Norton, 2013), p. 152.

146 **"Gaffer! If you think"**: Charles Dickens, *Our Mutual Friend* (1865; reprint, New York: Modern Library, 2002), p. 6.

Chapter 8: What's Up with the Apostrophe?

147 **"You would think that"**: Mark Twain, *The Innocents Abroad* (1869; reprint, New York: Signet Books/New American Library, 1966), p. 138.

148 **"whether there would be life"**: Gary Comer, "Before the Beginning and After," available at http://www.contentedshopper.com/clothing.htm.

151 **"The word or words that form"**: United States Board on Geographic Names, "Principles, Policies, and Procedures: Domestic Geographic Names." See http://geonames.usgs.gov/docs/pro_pol_pro.pdf.

152 **"an apostrophe-eradication policy"**: Barry Newman, "Theres a Question Mark Hanging over the Apostrophes Future," *Wall Street Journal*, May 15, 2013.

152 **"for some the possessive case"**: Kitty Burns Florey, *Sister Bernadette's Barking Dog: The Quirky History and the Lost Art of Diagramming Sentences* (Brooklyn, NY: Melville House Publishing, 2006), p. 77. (I am grateful to Burns Florey for digesting Gertrude Stein, "Poetry and Grammar," in *Lectures in America*.)

153 **"to avoid 'confusion'"**: BBC News, "Apostrophe Ban on Devon Council's New Street Names." See http://www.bbc.com/news/uk-england-devon-21795179.

153 **"the thought of apostrophes"**: Ibid.

Chapter 9: F*ck This Sh*t

161 **the rapper Earl Sweatshirt**: Kelefa Sanneh, "Where's Earl?" *The New Yorker*, May 23, 2011, pp. 59–67.

161 **"OMG Fucking Just Ran"**: Twitter post by Tyler, the Creator (Tyler Okonma), Sanneh, May 23, 2011.

161 **"there is *khuy* ('cock')"**: See http://www.newyorker.com/online/blogs/newsdesk/2014/05/vladimir-putins-four-dirty-words.html.

162 **"The term *mat* itself"**: Victor Erofeyev, "Dirty Words," *The New Yorker*, Sept. 15, 2003, p. 42.

162 **"the federal government could take"**: Calvin Trillin, "U.S. Letter: Atlanta," *The New Yorker*, Jan. 27, 1968, p. 102.

162 **report about a merchant marine**: John McPhee, "Looking for a Ship," *The New Yorker*, March 26, 1990.

162 **McPhee got his satisfaction**: John McPhee, "Editors and Publisher," *The New Yorker*, July 2, 2012, p. 34.

163 **"I've put more curse words"**: Booktalk Nation, Ian Frazier interviewed by Roy Blount Jr., December 6, 2012.

163 **the phrase "bros before hos"**: Ben McGrath, "Samba Soccer," *The New Yorker*, Jan. 13, 2014, p. 50.

Chapter 10: Ballad of a Pencil Junkie

187 **One of his principal sources**: *Logan (OH) Daily News*, March 18, 1999.

187 **"Nobody else does it"**: "Local Man's Collection of 2,393 Pencil Sharpeners on Display in His Museum," *Athens (OH) News*, June 17, 2003.

Appendix
....

SOME BOOKS I HAVE FOUND PARTICULARLY HELPFUL

Theodore Bernstein, the great stylist of the *New York Times*, has given us three collections of his judgments on what's fit to print: *Miss This-tlebottom's Hobgoblins: The Careful Writer's Guide to the Taboos, Bugbears and Outmoded Rules of English Usage* (Centro Books, 1971), *Dos, Don'ts & Maybes of English Usage* (Times Books, 1977), and *The Careful Writer: A Modern Guide to English Usage* (Atheneum, 1981). Authoritative, humane, and reassuring, Bernstein tells us, once and for all, that "none" is plural unless it means "not a single one."

Claire Kehrwald Cook, *Line by Line: How to Edit Your Own Writing* (Houghton Mifflin, 1985). A useful, concise manual with clear explanations and tips on (among other things) the difference between "further" and "farther," "a while" and "awhile," and "hanged" and "hung."

H. W. Fowler, *Fowler's Modern English Usage*, second edition, revised by Sir Ernest Gowers (whoever he was) (Oxford University Press, 1965). Originally compiled in 1926, H. W. Fowler's classic holds up well, not least because he's a good writer. Learn the difference between "flotsam" and "jetsam," and the subtle distinctions between "foam," "froth," and "scum." Not for use in an emergency.

Bryan Garner, *Garner's Modern American Usage*, third edition (Oxford University Press, 2009). A balanced and energetic usage guide from the American successor to Fowler. Exhaustive and inexhaustible, without being exhausting. If you read cookbooks for pleasure, that's what this is like: reflections on the ingredients of language.

Simon Heffer, *Strictly English: The Correct Way to Write . . . and Why It Matters* (Windmill Books, 2011). Almost a parody of a British curmudgeon, Heffer works for the *Daily Telegraph* and prides himself on his prescriptive ways. Useful as a corrective or if you need to know how to address a baronet.

Jack Lynch, *The Lexicographer's Dilemma: The Evolution of "Proper" English from Shakespeare to* South Park (Walker & Company, 2009). Best general introduction to the history of the language. Though Lynch clearly has a deep background, he leaves out the boring stuff.

David Marsh, *For Who the Bell Tolls* (Guardian Faber Publishing, 2013). This grew from a series of articles, posts, and tweets on *Guardian* style. Its guiding principle is Muphry's Law: "If you write anything criticising editing or proofreading, there will be a fault of some kind in what you have written." I take Marsh's point about "who" and "whom," but he should give John Donne his "m" back.

Henry Petroski, *The Pencil: A History of Design and Circumstance* (Knopf, 2011; originally published in 1989). An encyclopedic and enthusiastic survey of the humble writing tool, from the ancient Roman *penicillum* to pencil fanciers of our time.

Ammon Shea, *Bad English: A History of Linguistic Aggravation* (Penguin, 2014). Tolerant and amusing, Shea teaches us about such terms as "periphrastic" and "ligurition," defines Internet abbreviations ("brb") for oldsters, and debunks many a myth while promoting many another

(Nabokov liked smiley faces?). Also revives a commentator named Frank Vizetelly. Most optimistic book on our usage habits.

Marjorie E. Skillin and Robert M. Gay, *Words into Type*, third edition (Prentice-Hall, Inc., 1974). That's right, 1974. It may be pre-Internet, but it is still an indispensable reference book. A wise man once said, "You don't have to know everything about grammar, as long as you know where to look it up." *W.I.T.* is organized for this. I reach for it when I can't remember whether to italicize the genus or the species or which preposition goes with a particular verb.

William Strunk Jr. and E. B. White, *The Elements of Style*, third edition (Macmillan, 1979). In a mere eighty-five pages, Strunk and White offer timeless advice that generations have internalized. My copy has come apart between "Loan" ("A noun. As a verb, prefer *lend*") and "Meaningful" ("A bankrupt adjective"). For the insatiable, there is Mark Garvey's *Stylized: A Slightly Obsessive History of Strunk & White's* The Elements of Style (Simon and Schuster, 2009). It begins in 1918, with Professor Strunk privately publishing the "little book" for his students at Cornell. White rediscovered the book in 1957 and revised it three times. This account includes his correspondence with his editors and his readers as well as encomiums by appreciative writers.

Bill Walsh, the copy chief of the *Washington Post*, has composed a trilogy: *Lapsing into a Comma: A Curmudgeon's Guide to the Many Things That Can Go Wrong in Print—and How to Avoid Them* (Contemporary Books, 2000), *The Elephants of Style: A Trunkload of Tips on the Big Issues and Gray Areas of Contemporary American English* (McGraw Hill, 2004), and *Yes, I COULD Care Less: How to Be a Language Snob Without Being a Jerk* (St. Martin's Griffin, 2013). Walsh is down-to-earth and confident, an updated, folksier Bernstein.

INDEX

independent, 142
as objects, 89
relative, 39
restrictive and nonrestrictive,
39–42
Cleveland, Ohio, 73–74, 124, 186
author's youth in, 1–6, 27, 30, 72,
132–33, 182
Cleveland Costume Company,
author's job at, 2–3, 124
Cleveland Play House, 159
colash, 146
cold type, 112, 135
collating department, *The New
Yorker,* 42–47, 170–71, 198
*Collection of Essays and Fugitiv
Writings, A* (Webster), 25
colons, 71, 134, 135, 141, 145–46
and dashes, 145
semicolon vs., 145
Columbia University, 159
Comer, Gary, 148–49
"Coming into the Country"
(McPhee), 7–8
"comma fault," 110
commas, 55, 92–110, 129–30, 132,
135, 138, 142, 143, 152, 184,
199
between adjectives, 105–9
dashes as similar to, 134
misuse and overuse of, 96–97,
104, 107, 110
New Yorker style for, 46, 100–105
in nonrestrictive clauses, 39–42
origin of, 92, 103, 109
pairs of, 98–99, 134, 137
semicolons as similar to, 141
for separation of items, 40
commash, 146
"comma shaker," 46, 102, 197, 199
*Compendious Dictionary of the English
Language, A* (Webster), 25–26,
28
compound words:
en dashes in, 134
hyphens in, 47, 50–51, 114–18,
119–20
computers:
in publishing, 112–13, 135–36
word processing on, 133
conjunctions, commas and, 101,
142–43
Connecticut Magazine, 194

consistency:
in comma use, 94, 118
in hyphen use, 118
consonants:
doubling of, 16, 31, 49, 55, 198
sounds of, 18
context, 17
contractions, apostrophe use in,
153–54
"cooperate," "co-operate," "coöperate," 123
coordinate adjectives, 105–9
copulative verbs, 84, 86, 87, 88
copy editors, 35–38, 48–53, 70,
116–18, 122, 130, 135, 141, 154,
155, 193, 196
need for, 16–17
reputation of, 35–36
role of authors vs., 36, 46–56,
105, 108
see also specific individuals
Crosby, Miss, 169
Crow, Pat, 11, 50
Cursing Mommy, 163
Cyril, Saint, 25
Cyrillic alphabet, 25

Daily Show, The, 157
dairy industry, 3–6, 10
dangling participles, 52–54
dashes, 132–40
colons and, 145
Dickinson's use of, 137–40, 144–
45
double, 146
feminine slant of, 136–37
in pairs, 137, 145
placement of, 135–36
in profanity, 158
semicolons and, 143, 145
uses of, 134–35
"dashtards," 146
dates, en dashes in, 134
"Dear Frequent Travelers"
(Ephron), 49
Death on the Installment Plan (Céline),
131
definitions, 29
Delbanco, Andrew, 128–29
Derstein, Kristen-Lee, 185
descriptive clauses, *see* nonrestrictive
clauses
descriptivists, 19, 21, 68–69